California
Bed
&
Breakfast
Cookbook

California Bed & Breakfast Cookbook

First Edition

ISBN 1-889593-11-7

Printed in China

Design: Lisa Bachar & Tracey Ranta
Editing: Carol Faino & Susan Larson

Cover Photos: Richard Price (top)
Alison Miksch (bottom)

3D Press, Inc.
655 Broadway, Suite 560
Denver, CO 80203
303-623-4484 (phone)
303-623-4494 (fax)
info@3dpress.net

888-456-3607 (order toll-free)
www.3dpress.net

The Bed & Breakfast Cookbook Series™ was originated by Carol Faino & Doreen Hazledine of Peppermint Press in Denver, CO in 1996.

Introduction

The California Association of Bed & Breakfast Inns (CABBI) welcomes you to a taste of California. The more than 150 recipes featured in this inaugural CABBI cookbook are as flavorful and unique as the Golden State's distinct regions. From spicy south-of-the-border influences to time-honored recipes from Sierra mining towns to Wine Country creations to fresh seafood from the inns on the California coast, an epicurean experience at a CABBI bed & breakfast inn is long remembered.

Each recipe in this book was carefully chosen to tell the story of the inn from where it is served. Some recipes are house specialties, others are family heirlooms. Some dishes include locally-grown ingredients from an inn's region, while others are the reason guests return to an inn time and again. The bed and breakfast inn was born of sharing food and hospitality with friends. We hope that you will enjoy these CABBI favorites with your friends and loved ones, as we do with ours.

CABBI represents over 300 bed & breakfast inns throughout California's top five travel regions: Central Coast/Central Valley, Gold Country/High Sierra, Northern California, San Francisco Bay Area and Southern California. Every CABBI inn is inspected and certified to meet quality standards ensuring that all guests experience consistent customer service, amenities and the convenience of choice. For more information on CABBI bed and breakfast travel, see page 326 or visit us at www.cabbi.com. We look forward to welcoming you.

Bon appétit,

Teri Mattson
President, Board of Directors

CALIFORNIA ASSOCIATION OF BED & BREAKFAST INNS
A non-profit trade organization

About the Authors

Melissa Craven was the oldest child in a career Air Force family. Her husband, Chad, is from the Bay Area,. They visit California often, leading to Melissa's fondness for the natural beauty and diverse food cultures the state offers. Because of her passion for wine, Melissa enjoys touring the California Wine Country – one of the most esteemed wine producing regions in the world. With experience in journalism, recipe testing, marketing and public relations she understands the need for clear and concise recipes. As a cook, she understands the joy that comes from creating meals for family and friends. She melds her knowledge and interests to create winning recipes. Melissa is also the author of the *Colorado Farmers' Market Cookbook, Virginia Bed & Breakfast Cookbook* and co-author of *Red White & Blue Ribbon 2004.* She will co-author the soon-to-be-released *California Bed & Breakfast Cookbook* and is also a contributing editor in the other Bed & Breakfast Cookbook Series cookbooks.

Jordan Salcito, a Colorado native, attended Haverford College in Pennsylvania, where she majored in English Literature. With a background in writing and a lifelong passion for cuisine, she has been able to merge her two loves in the California Bed & Breakfast Cookbook. Having spent time with friends and family in California, she loves the spectrum of rustic beauty and urban sophistication that California offers. Jordan has worked in restaurants as a bartender, host, server, manager and sous chef, and understands the love and joy that comes from creating a meal for others. This is Jordan's second cookbook – she is also co-author of *Red White & Blue Ribbon 2004.* She has also written restaurant reviews for The Denver Post and will co-author the soon-to-be-released *California Bed & Breakfast Cookbook.*

Table of Contents

Breads & Muffins

Breads
&
Muffins

Anderson Creek Inn

In a lovely valley near the Mendocino Coast, you will find the Anderson Creek Inn. This gracious, ranch-style inn sits on 16 acres near the town of Boonville. The inn tastefully blends the beauty of the Anderson Valley with warm hospitality.

Views encompass the valley's rolling hills, which are peppered with majestic, old oaks and lined with tall redwoods kept fresh by the early morning coastal fog. Each room is lovely in its own way. The Garden Room has wonderful views of the garden, the creek and the meadows.

INNKEEPERS:	Jim & Grace Minton
ADDRESS:	12050 Anderson Valley Way
	Boonville, California 95415
TELEPHONE:	(707) 895-3091; (800) 552-6202
E-MAIL:	innkeeper@andersoncreekinn.com
WEBSITE:	www.andersoncreekinn.com
ROOMS:	5 Rooms; Private baths
CHILDREN:	Children age 10 and older welcome
ANIMALS:	Not allowed; Resident dogs & cats
HANDICAPPED:	Not handicapped accessible
DIETARY NEEDS:	Will accommodate guests' special dietary needs

Pear Bread

Makes 2 Loaves

"We're fortunate to have wonderful old varieties of pear trees in Anderson Valley. This is a great use of an abundance of pears." ~ Innkeeper, Anderson Creek Inn

1¾   cups sugar
1   cup vegetable oil
3   large eggs
Grated zest of 2 lemons
2   teaspoons vanilla extract
3   cups all-purpose flour
1   teaspoon salt
1   teaspoon baking soda
½   teaspoon baking powder
¾   teaspoon cinnamon
¼   teaspoon mace
4   pears, peeled and grated (about 3 cups)
¾   cup chopped pecans

Preheat oven to 350°F. In a large bowl, beat together sugar, oil and eggs. Add lemon zest and vanilla. Sift together flour, salt, baking soda, baking powder, cinnamon and mace into a medium bowl. Stir flour mixture into egg mixture. Stir in grated pears and pecans. Pour batter into 2 greased 9x5-inch glass loaf pans. Bake for 50 minutes, or until a toothpick inserted in center comes out clean.

Rose Mountain Manor

Set on five wooded acres in historic Colfax, Rose Mountain Manor is filled with charm and small town atmosphere. Located in the Sierra Foothills, the inn is within a 15-minute drive of Auburn, Grass Valley and Nevada City. Escape from life's daily stresses with home-style hospitality in quiet, luxurious accommodations.

Away from the hustle and bustle, you'll find the quaint Victorian tea room or the garden gazebo is the perfect place to enjoy a fine cup of tea and homemade scones and tea breads.

INNKEEPERS:	Barbara Bowers
ADDRESS:	233 Plutes Way
	Colfax, California 95713
TELEPHONE:	(530) 346-0067; (866) 444-7673
E-MAIL:	innkeeper@rosemountainmanor.com
WEBSITE:	www.rosemountainmanor.com
ROOMS:	3 Rooms; Private baths
CHILDREN:	Call ahead
ANIMALS:	Not allowed
HANDICAPPED:	Not handicapped accessible
DIETARY NEEDS:	Will accommodate guests' special dietary needs

Mango Bread

Makes 1 Loaf

2	cups all-purpose flour
2	teaspoons baking soda
½	teaspoon salt
2	teaspoons cinnamon
3	large eggs, beaten
1½	cups sugar
⅔	cup vegetable oil
1½	cups chopped mango
½	cup chopped nuts or raisins (optional)

Preheat oven to 350°F. In a large bowl, combine flour, baking soda, salt and cinnamon; make a well in the center. In a medium bowl, combine eggs, sugar, oil and mango. Pour egg mixture into well in flour mixture and mix until thoroughly combined. Stir in nuts or raisins, if desired. Pour batter into a greased 9x5-inch loaf pan. Bake for 1 hour, or until a toothpick inserted in center comes out clean.

The Beazley House

The Beazley House, located in the center of historic downtown Napa, is just steps from the trolley to Copia, Victorian neighborhoods, the Napa River, gourmet restaurants and premium outlet shopping. The Beazley House, with its central location for exploring wineries and the surrounding Wine Country, is the perfect Napa Valley bed & breakfast.

Elegant, yet comfortable guest rooms have private baths and garden views. The romantic Carriage House offers true Napa-style luxury with whirlpool tubs, fireplaces and complete privacy in hide-away rooms.

INNKEEPERS:	Jim & Carol Beazley
ADDRESS:	1910 First Street
	Napa, California 94559
TELEPHONE:	(707) 257-1649; (800) 559-1649
E-MAIL:	jim@beazleyhouse.com
WEBSITE:	www.beazleyhouse.com
ROOMS:	11 Rooms; Private baths
CHILDREN:	Welcome
ANIMALS:	Dogs & cats welcome; Resident dogs & cat
HANDICAPPED:	Handicapped accessible
DIETARY NEEDS:	Will accommodate guests' special dietary needs

Pineapple Bread

Makes 3 Loaves

2	tablespoons canola oil
2	cups sugar
3	large eggs
2	teaspoons vanilla extract
1	(20-ounce) can crushed pineapple, undrained
1	cup unsweetened applesauce
4½	cups unbleached all-purpose flour, divided
1	tablespoon baking soda
2	teaspoons baking powder
1	cup low-fat buttermilk
1	tablespoon cinnamon

Preheat oven to 325°F. In a large bowl, combine oil, sugar, eggs, vanilla, pineapple and applesauce. In a small bowl, combine 2½ cups of flour, baking soda and baking powder; add to pineapple mixture and stir until smooth and combined. Stir in buttermilk, cinnamon and remaining 2 cups of flour. Spray 3 (9x5-inch) loaf pans; 3 small Bundt pans; or 1 large and 1 small Bundt pan with non-stick cooking spray. Fill pans ⅔-full. Bake for 45 minutes, or until a toothpick inserted in center comes out clean.

Secret Garden Inn & Cottages

Secluded behind high hedges, hidden pathways and romantic gardens, lies the Secret Garden Inn & Cottages. Built for a large family in 1905, the house is now a delightful inn. Enjoy the Mediterranean climate while indulging in a leisurely breakfast served in bed, in the privacy of your garden patio or beneath the lacy, intertwined branches of the persimmon and avocado trees.

Delicious buffet breakfasts include freshly baked scones and muffins, special fruit dishes and quiches.

INNKEEPERS:	Dominique Hannaux
ADDRESS:	1908 Bath Street
	Santa Barbara, California 93101
TELEPHONE:	(805) 687-2300; (800) 676-1622
E-MAIL:	garden@secretgarden.com
WEBSITE:	www.secretgarden.com
ROOMS:	11 Rooms; 3 Suites; 9 Cottages; Private baths
CHILDREN:	Welcome
ANIMALS:	Dogs & cats welcome in cottages
HANDICAPPED:	Not handicapped accessible
DIETARY NEEDS:	Will accommodate guests' special dietary needs

Persimmon & Orange Nut Bread

Makes 2 Loaves

"We have a persimmon tree in the garden, and our guests love it when we cook with the fresh persimmons. This bread can be stored in the freezer for up to two months" ~ Innkeeper, Secret Garden Inn & Cottages

3½	cups all-purpose flour
2	cups brown sugar
2	teaspoons baking powder
1	teaspoon baking soda
½	teaspoon salt
1½	teaspoons cinnamon
½	teaspoon nutmeg
3	eggs
1	cup vegetable oil
½	cup orange juice
½	cup grated orange zest
2	cups persimmon pulp*
1	cup golden raisins
1	cup chopped nuts

Preheat oven to 325°F. In a large bowl, combine flour, brown sugar, baking powder, baking soda, salt, cinnamon and nutmeg. In a medium bowl, beat together eggs, oil, orange juice, orange zest and persimmon pulp. Add egg mixture to flour mixture; stir until combined. Stir in raisins and nuts. Pour batter into 2 well greased 9x5-inch loaf pans. Bake for 50 minutes, or until a toothpick inserted in center comes out clean. Cool on a wire rack.

*Note: Persimmons are available from October to February.

The Daughter's Inn

The Daughter's Inn is a landmark mansion in Old Town Napa. The inn is conveniently located on the trolley line to Copia and the Napa Valley Wine Train and is within walking distance of gourmet restaurants, the opera house and shopping. The inn's exquisite English gardens offer an idyllic retreat for guests to sit and reflect on a perfect day spent wine tasting in the world-renowned Napa Valley Wine Country.

"My first B&B experience was the Daughter's Inn, and it was incredible. Much better than any Ritz or Four Seasons I've ever stayed in." ~ Guest

INNKEEPERS:	Brooke Peterson
ADDRESS:	1938 First Street
	Napa, California 94559
TELEPHONE:	(866) 253-1331
E-MAIL:	innkeeper@daughtersinn.com
WEBSITE:	www.daughtersinn.com
ROOMS:	10 Rooms; Private baths
CHILDREN:	Children age 12 and older welcome
ANIMALS:	Not allowed
HANDICAPPED:	Handicapped accessible
DIETARY NEEDS:	Will accommodate guests' special dietary needs

Banana Almond Bread

Makes 3 Loaves

2	tablespoons canola oil
2	cups sugar
3	large eggs
2	teaspoons vanilla extract
2½	cups puréed or mashed very ripe banana
1¼	cups low-fat buttermilk
4	cups all-purpose flour, divided
1	tablespoon baking soda
1	teaspoon baking powder
⅓	cup chopped almonds

Preheat oven to 325°F. In a large bowl, combing oil, sugar, eggs, vanilla and bananas; mix thoroughly. Stir in buttermilk. In a medium bowl, combine flour, baking soda and baking powder. Stir flour mixture into banana mixture, a little at a time, until well combined. Stir in almonds.

Pour batter into 3 (9x5-inch) loaf pans; 1 large and 1 small Bundt pan; or 3 small Bundt pans sprayed with non-stick cooking spray. Bake for 45 minutes, or until a toothpick inserted in center comes out clean.

Oak Hill Manor

The Oak Hill Manor, built in 1984, is a 6,000-square-foot home that has been completely renovated by innkeepers Maurice and Risë Macaré. This elegant inn contains three suites, each with a fireplace and a whirlpool or claw-foot tub. Common areas include a formal parlor, pub, library, sun room, steam bath and other luxurious amenities.

Innkeeper Risë Macaré decorated each suite using unique European country styles. The inn was honored for having the "Best Interior Design and Decor" in Arrington's Bed & Breakfast Journal's 2003 Book of Lists.

INNKEEPERS:	Maurice & Risë Macaré
ADDRESS:	12345 Hampton Court
	Atascadero, California 93422
TELEPHONE:	(805) 462-9317; (866) 625-6267
E-MAIL:	macare@oakhillmanorbandb.com
WEBSITE:	www.oakhillmanorbandb.com
ROOMS:	8 Suites; Private baths
CHILDREN:	Welcome
ANIMALS:	Not allowed; Resident cat
HANDICAPPED:	Handicapped accessible
DIETARY NEEDS:	Will accommodate guests' special dietary needs

Butterscotch Banana Bread

Makes 2 Loaves

"This delicious recipe is adapted from the Toll House Heritage Cookbook. *The recipe can easily be halved." ~ Innkeeper, Oak Hill Manor Bed & Breakfast*

2	cups mashed ripe banana (about 4-6 bananas)
1½	cups sugar
1	stick butter, melted
2	large eggs
3½	cups all-purpose flour
4	teaspoons baking powder
1	teaspoon baking soda
1	teaspoon cinnamon
1	teaspoon salt
1	teaspoon nutmeg
½	cup milk
2⅔	cups chopped pecans, divided
1	(12-ounce) package Nestlé butterscotch morsels

Preheat oven to 350°F. In a large bowl, cream together bananas, sugar, butter and eggs. In a small bowl, combine flour, baking powder, baking soda, salt, cinnamon and nutmeg. Gradually add flour mixture alternately with milk to banana mixture, mixing well after each addition. Stir in 2 cups of pecans and butterscotch morsels.

Divide batter between 2 greased and floured 9x5-inch loaf pans. Sprinkle with remaining ⅔ cup of pecans. Bake for 60-70 minutes, until a toothpick inserted in center comes out clean. Cool bread in pans for 15 minutes, then remove from pans to a wire rack.

Tiffany Country House

The Tiffany Country House is a striking Victorian mansion located on a tree-lined street. The inn is just a short walk from Santa Barbara with its museums, art galleries and restaurants. Luxurious bedrooms include queen-size beds, whirlpool baths and large, open windows. The penthouse suite is a gorgeous, full-floor room with a fireplace, private balcony and spectacular mountain views.

The Taste of Romance Package includes champagne and a gift certificate for dinner at Louie's, one of Santa Barbara's best-loved restaurants.

INNKEEPERS:	Jan Martin Winn
ADDRESS:	1323 De La Vina Street
	Santa Barbara, California 93101
TELEPHONE:	(805) 963-2283; (800) 999-5672
E-MAIL:	innkeeper@tiffanycountryhouse.com
WEBSITE:	www.tiffanycountryhouse.com
ROOMS:	7 Rooms; Private baths
CHILDREN:	Children age 16 and older welcome
ANIMALS:	Not allowed
HANDICAPPED:	Not handicapped accessible
DIETARY NEEDS:	Will accommodate guests' special dietary needs

Chocolate Brioche Loaf

Makes 2 Loaves

"I adapted this recipe from one in Gourmet *magazine. It is a very dense bread with a great flavor – good for breakfast or afternoon tea." ~ Innkeeper, Tiffany ..ry House*

2½	cups all-purpose flour
⅔	cup unsweetened cocoa powder
1½	teaspoons baking powder
¾	teaspoon salt
2	large eggs, slightly beaten
1½	cups sugar
¾	stick butter, melted and cooled
1	cup sour cream
2	tablespoons brewed coffee, cooled
1	tablespoon vanilla extract
1	cup dried cranberries
1	cup chopped walnuts

Preheat oven to 350°F. In a large bowl, whisk together flour, cocoa, baking powder and salt. In a medium bowl, combine eggs, sugar, melted butter, sour cream, coffee and vanilla. Stir egg mixture into flour mixture, a little at a time, until combined. Fold in cranberries and nuts.

Pour batter into 2 greased 9x5-inch loaf pans. Smooth top of batter with a rubber spatula. Bake for 45-50 minutes, or until a toothpick inserted in center comes out clean or just slightly "wet." Cool loaves in pans for 10 minutes, then remove from pans and cool completely.

Carriage Vineyards

Situated on a 100-acre ranch near Paso Robles, Carriage Vineyards Bed & Breakfast is ideal for those seeking a peaceful country retreat. The inn's name is derived from the property's vineyards and the innkeepers' carriage collection.

Wander amidst 20,000 grape vines planted on 27 acres. The inn is home to 500 olive trees and a 2,400-square-foot carriage house sheltering 12 antique carriages. Relax with a book under a tree in the small orchard or find peace of mind in the vegetable garden, flower gardens and sitting areas.

INNKEEPERS:	Larry & Diane Smyth & Joanna & Mike Caldwell
ADDRESS:	4337 South El Pomar Road
	Templeton, California 93465
TELEPHONE:	(800) 617-7911
E-MAIL:	joannalc@aol.com
WEBSITE:	www.carriagevineyards.com
ROOMS:	3 Rooms; 3 Suites; Private & shared baths
CHILDREN:	Children age 12 and older welcome
ANIMALS:	Horses welcome; Resident horses
HANDICAPPED:	Not handicapped accessible
DIETARY NEEDS:	Cannot accommodate guests' special dietary needs

Barbecued Olive Bread

Makes 2 Loaves

"We have approximately 500 olive trees on the property. This bread, which is actually grilled, is a way to use some of our annual olive harvest." ~ Innkeeper, Carriage Vineyards Bed & Breakfast

1	(4-ounce) can chopped ripe olives
½	cup chopped pimento-stuffed olives
¾	cup grated colby Jack cheese
½	cup plus 4 tablespoons grated Parmesan cheese, divided
½	stick butter, melted
1	tablespoon olive oil
2	cloves garlic, minced
3	drops hot pepper sauce
2	cups biscuit mix (such as Bisquick)
⅔	cup milk
2	tablespoons minced fresh parsley

Paprika

Preheat grill. In a small bowl, combine ripe and pimento-stuffed olives, colby Jack cheese, ½ cup of Parmesan cheese, melted butter, olive oil, garlic and hot pepper sauce; set aside.

In a medium bowl, combine biscuit mix, milk, 2 tablespoons of Parmesan cheese and parsley; stir until moist, then press into 2 (9-inch) disposable aluminum pie pans. Top dough with olive mixture. Sprinkle with paprika and remaining 2 tablespoons of Parmesan cheese.

Grill bread over indirect heat, covered, for 8-10 minutes, or until crust is golden brown when edge of bread is lifted with a spatula.

Mission Inn

The Mission Inn is an early California, Hacienda-style inn nestled in the coastal Capistrano Valley between the Pacific Ocean and the Cleveland National Forest. The inn is located in a two acre, century-old family orchard adjacent to the historic Mission San Juan Capistrano. The melodic sound of the mission's bells can be heard while strolling through historic San Juan, as you read by the inn's pool or sip sherry on the veranda.

Patio rooms have a patio for private outdoor lounging under one of the orchard's orange trees – you can pick a fresh orange any time you desire!

INNKEEPERS:	Jory Brashier & Droze Kern
ADDRESS:	26891 Ortega Highway
	San Juan Capistrano, California 92675
TELEPHONE:	(949) 234-0249; (866) 234-0249
E-MAIL:	innkeeper@missioninnsjc.com
WEBSITE:	www.missioninnsjc.com
ROOMS:	18 Rooms; 2 Suites; Private baths
CHILDREN:	Welcome
ANIMALS:	Welcome
HANDICAPPED:	Handicapped accessible
DIETARY NEEDS:	Will accommodate guests' special dietary needs

Sarah's Mississippi Buttermilk Biscuits

Makes 8 Large or 10 Small Biscuits

2   cups self-rising all-purpose flour
1   cup buttermilk
½   cup canola oil
Butter or margarine, for serving
Preserves or honey, for serving

Preheat oven to 400°F. Mix flour, buttermilk and oil until moist. Roll out dough and cut with a biscuit cutter or a glass. Place biscuits in a cast-iron skillet or a greased baking pan. Bake for 20 minutes, or until tops are golden brown. Serve piping hot with butter or margarine and your favorite preserves or honey.

Roundstone Farm

Welcome to Roundstone Farm, a serene place where guests enjoy the company of new friends, delightful breakfasts and the sights and sounds of the natural surroundings. Ever changing panoramic views of Mt. Wittenberg, Olema Valley, Inverness Ridge and Tomales Bay provide a visual feast for inn guests. Enveloped in ten acres of rolling hills, the inn is located in the small town of Olema, on the northern coast of California.

Within minutes of the inn, the Point Reyes National Seashore has hundreds of miles of trails and over 20 pristine ocean and bay beaches.

INNKEEPERS:	Karen Anderson & Frank Borodic
ADDRESS:	9940 Sir Francis Drake Boulevard
	Olema, California 94950
TELEPHONE:	(415) 663-1020; (800) 881-9874
E-MAIL:	info@roundstonefarm.com
WEBSITE:	www.roundstonefarm.com
ROOMS:	5 Rooms; Private baths
CHILDREN:	Welcome
ANIMALS:	Not allowed
HANDICAPPED:	Not handicapped accessible
DIETARY NEEDS:	Will accommodate guests' special dietary needs

Sesame Seed Corn Bread

Makes 2 Loaves

1½	cups all-purpose flour
½	cup sugar
1	teaspoon baking soda
1	cup polenta
½	cup yellow cornmeal
¾	cup wheat germ
½	cup sesame seeds, plus extra for topping
½	cup canola oil
1½	cups buttermilk
3	eggs

Preheat oven to 350°F. In a large bowl, combine flour, sugar, baking soda, polenta, yellow cornmeal, wheat germ and sesame seeds. In a medium bowl, combine oil, buttermilk and eggs. Add egg mixture to polenta mixture; mix until well combined. Fill 2 greased 9x5-inch loaf pans ⅔-full with batter. Sprinkle tops of loaves with sesame seeds. Bake for 50-60 minutes, or until a toothpick inserted in center comes out clean. Cool bread in pans, then turn out onto a wire rack.

Auberge Mendocino

AUBERGE MENDOCINO

The Auberge Mendocino, overlooking Little River Bay on the rugged Northern California coast, offers comfort with style in a setting of exceptional beauty. Just outside historic Mendocino, the inn is nestled between two California state parks. Whale watching, hiking and water sports are at your door. The Mendocino Wine Country and Noyo Harbor at Fort Bragg are just a few miles down scenic California Highway One.

A scrumptious breakfast may include scrambled eggs with smoked salmon, home fries with dill rémoulade sauce and boysenberry scone cake.

INNKEEPERS:	Richard Grabow
ADDRESS:	8200 Highway 1
	Little River, California 95465
TELEPHONE:	(707) 937-0088; (800) 347-9252
E-MAIL:	innkeeper@aubergemendocino.com
WEBSITE:	www.aubergemendocino.com
ROOMS:	11 Rooms; Private baths
CHILDREN:	Welcome
ANIMALS:	Not allowed
HANDICAPPED:	Handicapped accessible; 1 room
DIETARY NEEDS:	Will accommodate guests' special dietary needs

Cranberry Pecan Eggnog Muffins

Makes 8 Muffins

"I think eggnog has a wonderful flavor – and it is more versatile than people realize. I use it as a substitute liquid in several recipes I have created for the holidays. This recipe is from Rachel's Heritage Collection, a collection of recipes from the inn's former owner. It combines the tartness of cranberries with the sweet richness of eggnog." - Innkeeper, Auberge Mendocino

2½	cups all-purpose flour
½	cup plus 3 tablespoons sugar
Scant ½	teaspoon salt
2	teaspoons baking powder
½	teaspoon nutmeg
1	heaping cup coarsely chopped pecans
1	cup eggnog
1	large egg
½	stick butter, melted (or ¼ cup vegetable oil), plus extra for greasing muffin cups
2	teaspoons vanilla extract
1	teaspoon rum flavoring or ¾ teaspoon light rum
1	heaping cup fresh or frozen cranberries

Preheat oven to 375°F. In a large bowl, combine flour, sugar, salt, baking powder, nutmeg and pecans. In a small bowl, combine eggnog, egg, butter, vanilla, rum flavoring and cranberries. Combine flour mixture and eggnog mixture using as few strokes as possible (overbeating can cause muffins to toughen and have air tunnels).

Grease muffin cups liberally with butter. Fill muffin cups ⅔-full. Bake for 30-40 minutes, or until a toothpick inserted in center comes out clean and muffins are slightly golden brown on top.

Holly Tree Inn

The Holly Tree Inn is located in a secluded 19-acre valley surrounded by wooded hillsides, adjacent to Point Reyes National Seashore. On the sunny mesa above the inn are expansive organic flower and vegetable gardens and a greenhouse, from which the ingredients in many of the inn's savory and hearty breakfasts are taken.

Room amenities include fresh flowers, luxurious robes, hot tubs and fireplaces. Choose from a room in the 1939 inn or a cottage in a wooded setting or on a pier over the waters of Tomales Bay.

INNKEEPERS: Tom Balogh
ADDRESS: 3 Silverhills Road
     Point Reyes Station, California 94956
TELEPHONE: (415) 663-1554; (800) 286-4655
E-MAIL: info@hollytreeinn.com
WEBSITE: www.hollytreeinn.com
ROOMS: 4 Rooms; 3 Cottages; Private baths
CHILDREN: Welcome
ANIMALS: Not allowed; Resident dog & cats
HANDICAPPED: Not handicapped accessible
DIETARY NEEDS: Will accommodate guests' special dietary needs

Ginger Banana Nut Muffins

Makes 12 Muffins

½	cup vegetable oil
1	cup packed brown sugar
3	very ripe bananas, mashed
2	large eggs
3	tablespoons buttermilk
1	teaspoon vanilla extract
2	cups all-purpose flour
1	teaspoon baking soda
½	teaspoon salt
½	teaspoon baking powder
½	cup chopped pecans, or more to taste
⅓	cup chopped candied ginger
½	teaspoon nutmeg
¼	teaspoon powdered ginger
½	teaspoon cinnamon (optional)

Preheat oven to 350°F. In a large bowl, combine oil, brown sugar, bananas, eggs, buttermilk and vanilla. In a medium bowl, combine flour, baking soda, salt, baking powder, pecans, candied ginger, nutmeg, powdered ginger and cinnamon. Add flour mixture to banana mixture; mix well. Divide batter among greased or paper-lined muffin cups. Bake for 20-25 minutes.

The Inn at Schoolhouse Creek

E xperience the true luxury of solitude at this Mendocino coast inn. Set on eight acres of ocean-view gardens, meadows, forest and a secluded beach cove, you will truly feel like you've gotten away from it all. The Inn at Schoolhouse Creek offers privacy and a carefree atmosphere where you can enjoy your vacation on your own schedule. Sit in the gardens or watch the waves break and whales spout from your cottage.

The charming and historic village of Mendocino, with its many fine shops, galleries and restaurants, is five minutes from the inn.

INNKEEPERS:	Steven Musser & Maureen Gilbert
ADDRESS:	7051 North Highway One
	Mendocino, California 95456
TELEPHONE:	(707) 937-5525; (800) 731-5525
E-MAIL:	innkeeper@schoolhousecreek.com
WEBSITE:	www.schoolhousecreek.com
ROOMS:	4 Rooms; 2 Suites; 9 Cottages; Private baths
CHILDREN:	Welcome
ANIMALS:	Welcome; Resident dogs
HANDICAPPED:	Handicapped accessible
DIETARY NEEDS:	Will accommodate guests' special dietary needs

Apple Cheddar Muffins with Rosemary

Makes 12 Muffins

1½	cups all-purpose flour
¼	cup old-fashioned rolled oats
1	tablespoon sugar
2	teaspoons baking powder
½	teaspoon baking soda
½	teaspoon salt
⅛	teaspoon white pepper
⅛	teaspoon cardamom
¼	teaspoon allspice
½	teaspoon minced fresh rosemary
¾	cup skim milk
2	eggs, beaten
½	stick unsalted butter, melted
1	large Granny Smith or pippin apple, peeled and cut into ⅛-inch dice
¾	cup grated sharp white cheddar cheese

Preheat oven to 400°F. In a large bowl, combine flour, oats, sugar, baking powder, baking soda, salt, white pepper, cardamom, allspice and rosemary. In a medium bowl, whisk together milk, eggs and melted butter. Stir apples and cheese into egg mixture. Add egg mixture to flour mixture and stir just until blended.

Pour batter into greased muffin cups. Bake for 15-20 minutes, or until a toothpick inserted in center comes out clean. Cool muffins in pan for 3 minutes, then remove muffins to a wire rack.

Union Street Inn

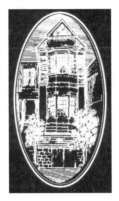

Experience warm European hospitality in San Francisco's elegant Union Street Inn. Combining the elegance and gentility of an Edwardian home, the inn is the perfect pied-à-terre for those wanting to explore San Francisco. Rooms are spacious, airy and comfortably furnished. Antique accents, fresh flowers and pleasing artworks create a sense of the romantic.

Open the window and the fragrance of old roses, lavender, sage and rosemary wafts up from the cottage garden – a delightful spot to enjoy an delectable breakfast or afternoon tea.

INNKEEPERS:	Jane Bertorelli & David Coyle
ADDRESS:	2229 Union Street
	San Francisco, California 94123
TELEPHONE:	(415) 346-0424
E-MAIL:	innkeeper@unionstreetinn.com
WEBSITE:	www.unionstreetinn.com
ROOMS:	6 Rooms; Private baths
CHILDREN:	Welcome
ANIMALS:	Not allowed; Resident dog & cat
HANDICAPPED:	Not handicapped accessible
DIETARY NEEDS:	Will accommodate guests' special dietary needs

Raspberry Almond Muffins

Makes 12 Jumbo Muffins

3	cups all-purpose flour
⅔	cup sugar
2	teaspoons salt
2	teaspoons baking powder
2	teaspoons baking soda
2	cups raspberries
2	large eggs
2	tablespoons almond extract
¼	cup canola oil
1¼	cups buttermilk (about)

Sliced almonds

Preheat oven to 375°F. Line 12 jumbo muffin cups with paper liners or spray with non-stick cooking spray. In a bowl, combine flour, sugar, salt, baking powder and baking soda. Gently stir in raspberries.

Beat eggs in a 2-cup measuring cup. Mix almond extract and oil into eggs. Add enough buttermilk to egg mixture to make 2 cups of liquid. Add egg mixture to flour mixture; stir gently just until combined. Divide batter among muffin cups. Sprinkle with almonds. Bake for 30 minutes, until firm to the touch.

Coffee Cakes, Scones, Granola & Oatmeal

Coffee Cakes, Scones, Granola & Oatmeal

Tiffany Country House

Entering the Tiffany Country House means entering a world of timeless romance. The front entry sets the tone with antique furnishings and quiet elegance. Tea is served each afternoon in the parlor, with its lovely period furniture, inviting fireplace and views of the inn's lush gardens.

The Victoria Room has a whirlpool tub, queen-size bed with mahogany headboard and French doors that open onto a view of the rose garden. A wood-burning fireplace warms the room's ivory and floral tones.

INNKEEPERS:	Jan Martin Winn
ADDRESS:	1323 De La Vina Street
	Santa Barbara, California 93101
TELEPHONE:	(805) 963-2283; (800) 999-5672
E-MAIL:	innkeeper@tiffanycountryhouse.com
WEBSITE:	www.tiffanycountryhouse.com
ROOMS:	7 Rooms; Private baths
CHILDREN:	Children age 16 and older welcome
ANIMALS:	Not allowed
HANDICAPPED:	Not handicapped accessible
DIETARY NEEDS:	Will accommodate guests' special dietary needs

Sour Cream Banana Toffee Crumb Cake

Makes 1 Cake

"This recipe is adapted from one in Food & Wine *magazine. It is simple and delicious." – Innkeeper, Tiffany Country House*

2¾	cups all-purpose flour
2½	teaspoons baking powder
½	teaspoon baking soda
½	teaspoon salt
1½	sticks butter, softened
1½	cups sugar
3	large eggs
1½	teaspoons vanilla extract
1	cup sour cream
½	cup mashed ripe banana

Toffee topping:

½	cup coarsely chopped chocolate-covered English toffee (such as Skor or Heath bar)
⅓	cup all-purpose flour
¼	cup powdered sugar
2	tablespoons butter

Preheat oven to 350°F. In a medium bowl, whisk together flour, baking powder, baking soda and salt. In a large bowl, beat butter and sugar with a mixer until light and fluffy. Beat in eggs and vanilla. Beat in sour cream and banana until smooth. Beat in flour mixture until smooth.

Pour batter into a greased, 10-inch springform pan. Sprinkle toffee topping over batter. Bake for 70 minutes, or until a toothpick inserted in center comes out clean. Cool cake slightly in pan, then remove outer rim from pan and cool cake completely.

For the toffee topping: Combine topping ingredients until crumbly.

Glenelly Inn & Cottages

The Glenelly Inn & Cottages is a historic and traditional circa 1916 bed & breakfast inn offering leisurely graciousness and country hospitality in the heart of the Sonoma Wine Country.

The innkeepers will pack a picnic lunch for two with sandwiches such as tri-tip beef with sun-dried tomatoes, garlic olive oil and green peppercorn mustard, grilled chicken with tarragon mustard or Brie and roasted peppers with lemon olive oil and spicy Provençal mustard. Also included is a Glenelly cooler bag, opener and two wine glasses for you to take home.

INNKEEPERS:	Kristi Hallamore Jeppesen
ADDRESS:	5131 Warm Springs Road
	Glen Ellen, California 95442
TELEPHONE:	(707) 996-6720
E-MAIL:	glenelly@glenelly.com
WEBSITE:	www.glenelly.com
ROOMS:	6 Rooms; 2 Suites; 2 Cottages; Private baths
CHILDREN:	Welcome
ANIMALS:	Not allowed; Resident dogs & cat
HANDICAPPED:	Handicapped accessible
DIETARY NEEDS:	Will accommodate guests' special dietary needs

Espresso Coffee Cake a.k.a. Kaelene's Kona Coffee Cake

Makes 8 to 10 Servings

This is a quick and delicious Cake Mix Doctor-type coffee cake.

4	large eggs
1	stick butter, melted
1	cup sour cream
1	(18-ounce) package yellow cake mix
½	cup packed brown sugar
½	cup instant coffee powder (espresso, regular or decaf)

Powdered sugar, for garnish

Preheat oven to 375°F. In a bowl, beat eggs lightly. Stir in butter and sour cream. Add cake mix, brown sugar and coffee powder; mix thoroughly. Pour batter into a greased and floured Bundt pan.

Bake for 40 minutes, or until a toothpick inserted in center comes out clean. Cool cake in pan for 5-10 minutes, then turn out onto a wire rack and cool completely. Dust cooled cake with powdered sugar to serve.

Chelsea Garden Inn

In the Chelsea Garden Inn's private, latticed courtyard, with its tree-lined garden paths and secluded swimming pool, you'll feel as if you are miles from anywhere. It is a wonderful place to watch the seasons change. Yet, you are only two blocks from shops, restaurants, spas and wine tasting on historic Calistoga's Main Street.

The poolside social room, with its vaulted ceiling, large fireplace and wonderful library, is a favorite of inn guests. A delicious full breakfast is served each morning in the bistro-style dining room.

INNKEEPERS:	Diane Byrne
ADDRESS:	1443 Second Street
	Calistoga, California 94515
TELEPHONE:	(707) 942-0948; (800) 942-1515
E-MAIL:	innkeeper@chelseagardeninn.com
WEBSITE:	www.chelseagardeninn.com
ROOMS:	1 Rooms; 3 Suites; 1 Cottage; Private baths
CHILDREN:	Welcome
ANIMALS:	Not allowed
HANDICAPPED:	Not handicapped accessible
DIETARY NEEDS:	Will accommodate guests' special dietary needs

Strawberry Streusel Coffee Cake

Makes 8 Servings

"We serve this recipe for those special occasions when strawberries and white chocolate are called for!" - Innkeeper, Chelsea Garden Bed & Breakfast

1½	cups all-purpose flour
¾	cup sugar
¾	cup milk
2	teaspoons baking powder
½	stick butter or margarine, softened
1	large egg
2	cups sliced fresh or frozen strawberries

White chocolate streusel topping:

½	cup packed brown sugar
½	cup white baking chips
⅓	cup all-purpose flour
½	stick butter or margarine, softened

White chocolate glaze:

½	cup white baking chips
2	tablespoons light corn syrup
1½	teaspoons water

Preheat oven to 350°F. Grease and flour a 10-inch tube cake pan. Beat flour, sugar, milk, baking powder, butter and egg with a mixer on low speed just until moistened. Beat on medium speed for 1 minute, scraping bowl occasionally. Spread ⅔ of batter in pan. Top with strawberries. Carefully spread remaining batter over strawberries. Sprinkle streusel topping over batter. Bake for 55-65 minutes, until top is golden and a toothpick inserted in center comes out clean. Cool cake in pan for 10 minutes, then remove from pan. Drizzle glaze over warm cake. Serve warm.

For the streusel topping: Mix all streusel ingredients until crumbly.

For the glaze: Heat all glaze ingredients in a small saucepan over low heat, stirring constantly, until mixture is smooth and thin enough to drizzle.

Auberge Mendocino

AUBERGE
MENDOCINO

Informal gardens and century-old cypress trees surround Auberge Mendocino, a Northern California Wine Country inn on the rugged Mendocino coast. Historic Mendocino, famous for its water towers and the Mendocino Art Center, is just up the road. Enjoy outstanding local wines at one of eight award-winning restaurants within three miles of the inn.

The Grey Room has a dramatic view of the ocean, coastal headlands and the beach at Van Damme. The room also includes a comfortable sitting area with wing chairs for reading or enjoying the view.

INNKEEPERS:	Richard Grabow
ADDRESS:	Post Office Box 134
	Mendocino, California 95460
TELEPHONE:	(707) 937-0088; (800) 347-9252
E-MAIL:	innkeeper@aubergemendocino.com
WEBSITE:	www.aubergemendocino.com
ROOMS:	11 Rooms; Private baths
CHILDREN:	Welcome
ANIMALS:	Not allowed
HANDICAPPED:	Handicapped accessible; 1 room
DIETARY NEEDS:	Will accommodate guests' special dietary needs

Apricot Cream Cheese Coffee Cake

Makes 12 Servings

"This cake is also known as 'David's Cake,' named after my 5-year-old nephew who said, 'This is the best cake I've ever eaten in my whole life!' This recipe is from Rachel's Heritage Collection, a collection of recipes from the inn's former owner." ~ Innkeeper, Auberge Mendocino

1	stick butter, softened
½	cup sugar
Grated zest of 1 lemon	
2	large eggs
1	teaspoon vanilla extract
1	teaspoon baking powder
½	teaspoon salt
1	heaping cup unbleached all-purpose flour
10	apricots, halved and pitted (or plums)

Topping:

½	(8-ounce) package cream cheese, softened
½	cup sugar
2	tablespoons sour cream
1	large egg
1	teaspoon vanilla extract

Preheat oven to 350°F. In a large bowl, cream together butter, sugar and lemon zest. Beat in eggs, 1 at a time. Beat in vanilla. In a small bowl, combine baking powder, salt and flour; beat into butter mixture. Pour batter into a greased 9-inch springform pan. Place apricots skin-side-down on top of batter. Spread topping over apricots. Bake for about 1 hour, or until top is set and begins to brown.

For the topping: Beat cream cheese and sugar until smooth. Add sour cream, egg and vanilla; beat well.

Mayfield House at Lake Tahoe

Experience luxurious accommodations in Lake Tahoe at the Mayfield House. Enjoy the finest example of "Old Tahoe" architecture and charm. The inn is centrally located, close to hiking, biking, boating, great restaurants and shops. Walk to Lake Tahoe or drive ten minutes to world-class skiing at Alpine Meadows and Squaw Valley ski areas.

Enjoy a full, gourmet breakfast of homemade breads, such as banana chocolate chip granola, and delicious entrées such as cinnamon French toast with bananas and apple walnut pancakes with pure maple syrup.

INNKEEPERS:	Colleen McDevitt
ADDRESS:	236 Grove Street
	Tahoe City, California 96145
TELEPHONE:	(530) 583-1001; (888) 518-8898
E-MAIL:	innkeeper@mayfieldhouse.com
WEBSITE:	www.mayfieldhouse.com
ROOMS:	3 Rooms; 2 Suites; 1 Cottage; Private baths
CHILDREN:	Welcome
ANIMALS:	Dogs welcome in cottage
HANDICAPPED:	Not handicapped accessible
DIETARY NEEDS:	Will accommodate guests' special dietary needs

Merk's Coffee Cake

Makes 12 to 16 Servings

2	sticks butter or margarine
1¾	cups sugar
1	cup sour cream
2	eggs, beaten well
1	teaspoon vanilla extract
2	cups all-purpose flour
1	teaspoon baking powder
¼	teaspoon salt
½	teaspoon baking soda

Filling:

¾-1	cup chopped nuts
2½	teaspoons cinnamon
¼	cup sugar

Preheat oven to 350°F. In a large bowl, cream together butter, sugar and sour cream. Add eggs and vanilla; mix well. In a medium bowl, combine flour, baking powder, salt and baking soda; add to butter mixture and mix well.

Sprinkle ½ of filling into a well-greased and floured tube cake pan. Top with ½ of batter. Top with remaining filling, then with remaining batter. Bake for 45-55 minutes, until a toothpick inserted in center comes out clean. Cool cake in pan for 10 minutes, then remove from pan and cool completely on a wire rack.

For the filling: Combine nuts, cinnamon and sugar.

The Inn at Locke House

The Inn at **Locke House** Bed and Breakfast

Enjoy the romance, simple elegance and serenity of the historic Inn at Locke House, a rural home graced with English country gardens. From your room, gaze upon the Sierra foothills and countryside dotted with horse ranches, orchards and vineyards. Locke House is convenient to Lake Tahoe, Sierra Nevada resorts, Gold Country and Yosemite National Park.

A freshly baked "confection of the day," a variety of delectable nibbles and beverages welcome guests to the inn. Later, join the innkeepers for dessert in the parlor, carriageway or farmhands dining room.

INNKEEPERS:	Richard & Lani Eklund
ADDRESS:	19960 Elliott Road
	Lockeford, California 95237
TELEPHONE:	(209) 727-5715
E-MAIL:	lockehouse@jps.net
WEBSITE:	www.theinnatlockehouse.com
ROOMS:	4 Rooms; 1 Suite; Private baths
CHILDREN:	Children age 12 and older welcome
ANIMALS:	Not allowed
HANDICAPPED:	Not handicapped accessible
DIETARY NEEDS:	Will accommodate guests' special dietary needs

Grape Muffin Breakfast Cake

Makes 10 to 12 Servings

"Our Tokay grapevines produce the perfect size grapes for this coffee cake. Any small seedless grape works just as nicely as our Tokays. Our guests ask us to make enough for afternoon tea." ~ Innkeeper, The Inn at Locke House

Butter-flavored shortening
2   tablespoons plus ¾ cup sugar
2   tablespoons dry breadcrumbs
1½   cups unbleached all-purpose flour, sifted
2   teaspoons baking powder
1   teaspoon baking soda
½   teaspoon salt
2   teaspoons nutmeg
5⅓   tablespoons unsalted butter, chilled and diced
1   cup small seedless grapes
1   extra-large egg, slightly beaten
½   cup buttermilk
1   teaspoon vanilla extract
Powdered sugar, for garnish
Grape clusters and grape leaves, for garnish

Preheat oven to 350°F. Generously grease a large Bundt pan with shortening. Mix 2 tablespoons of sugar and breadcrumbs and use to dust pan.

Sift together ¾ cup of sugar, flour, baking powder, baking soda, salt and nutmeg into a large bowl. Cut in butter until mixture resembles coarse crumbs. Gently stir in grapes. In a small bowl, combine egg, buttermilk and vanilla. Add egg mixture to flour mixture; stir lightly until combined.

Spoon batter into pan and bake for 30-40 minutes, or until a toothpick inserted in center comes out clean (be careful not to overbake). Cool cake for 10 minutes in pan on a wire rack. Turn cake out onto a serving plate. Dust with powdered sugar. Garnish with grape clusters and leaves.

Old St. Angela Inn

The Old St. Angela Inn, born a country home in 1910 and converted to a rectory and then a convent in 1920, is now a cozy bed & breakfast inn overlooking Monterey Bay. Within this turn-of-the-century, shingle-style home are rooms of distinctive individuality and warmth that provide comfort and serenity.

The Old St. Angela Inn is 100 yards from the water and only minutes from excellent restaurants and shopping, world-class golf, Monterey's Old Cannery Row and the Monterey Bay Aquarium.

INNKEEPERS:	Sue Kuslis & Lew Shaefer
ADDRESS:	321 Central Avenue
	Pacific Grove, California 93950
TELEPHONE:	(831) 372-3246; (800) 748-6306
E-MAIL:	lew@redshift.com
WEBSITE:	www.sueandlewinns.com
ROOMS:	9 Rooms; Private baths
CHILDREN:	Children age 6 and older welcome
ANIMALS:	Not allowed
HANDICAPPED:	Handicapped accessible
DIETARY NEEDS:	Will accommodate guests' special dietary needs

Apple Pecan Brunch Pastry

Makes 12 Pastries

"This recipe was adapted from a winning recipe in the 1993 Pepperidge Farm Recipe Contest." - Innkeeper, Old St. Angela Inn

½   (17-ounce) package Pepperidge Farm puff pastry sheet (1 sheet)
1   cup packed brown sugar
½   cup all-purpose flour
1   teaspoon cinnamon
⅛   teaspoon nutmeg
2   cups diced, peeled Granny Smith apples (about 2 medium apples)
1   cup chopped pecans
1   tablespoon butter, chilled and cut into small pieces

Glaze:
½   cup powdered sugar
1½   teaspoons almond extract
2-3   teaspoons water

Thaw puff pastry sheet at room temperature for 30 minutes. Preheat oven to 375°F. In a large bowl, combine brown sugar, flour, cinnamon and nutmeg. Add apples, pecans and butter; toss to coat.

Unfold pastry on a lightly floured surface. Roll out into a 15x10-inch rectangle. Brush lightly with water. Spoon apple mixture over pastry to within 2-inches of long sides and to edge of short sides.

Starting with the long side, roll up pastry jelly-roll style. Cut dough into 12 (1¼-inch-thick) slices. Place slices 2 inches apart on a greased baking sheet. Bake for 15 minutes, or until golden. Remove pastries from baking sheet and cool slightly on a wire rack, then drizzle with glaze.

For the glaze: Mix all glaze ingredients, adding enough water to achieve desired consistency.

Channel Road Inn

The Channel Road Inn provides the comfortable elegance of a turn-of-the-century Santa Monica home and the timeless pleasure of a seashore retreat. This fully restored, circa 1915 manor is located only one block from the glorious Santa Monica beach in Santa Monica Canyon, an exclusive, yet eclectic and rustic section of Los Angeles.

When you are ready to re-join the pulse of the city, some of the area's best dining, shopping and entertainment are within five minutes. Ride, jog or walk south to the Santa Monica Pier, or drive along the coast to Malibu.

INNKEEPERS:	Christine L. Marwell
ADDRESS:	219 West Channel Road
	Santa Monica, California 90402
TELEPHONE:	(310) 459-1920
E-MAIL:	info@channelroadinn.com
WEBSITE:	www.channelroadinn.com
ROOMS:	14 Rooms; 1 Suite; Private baths
CHILDREN:	Welcome
ANIMALS:	Not allowed
HANDICAPPED:	Handicapped accessible
DIETARY NEEDS:	Will accommodate guests' special dietary needs

Cream Scones with Berries

Makes 12 Scones

2   cups all-purpose flour
1   tablespoon sugar, plus extra for topping
1   tablespoon baking powder
1   stick butter, chilled and cut into small pieces
2   eggs
½   cup heavy cream
1½   teaspoons vanilla extract
1   cup fresh or frozen berries of choice
Egg wash (1 egg yolk beaten with 1 tablespoon of water or milk)

Preheat oven to 350°F. In a large bowl, combine flour, sugar and baking powder. Cut in butter until mixture resembles a coarse meal. In a medium bowl, combine eggs, cream and vanilla. Stir cream mixture into flour mixture until flour is incorporated, then mix for 1-2 minutes longer. Add berries and mix gently just until combined.

With an ice cream scoop, scoop batter onto a parchment paper-lined baking sheet. Brush scones with a little egg wash and sprinkle with sugar. Bake for 30-40 minutes, or until golden brown on top.

Alegria Oceanfront Inn

Alegria, which means the state of being joyful and happy, is an inn that welcomes you by putting your cares to rest and applying attention to every detail of your stay. The innkeepers want you to focus on more important things – the hummingbird out the window, the fragrance of the ocean breeze or the sunlight across the garden path leading to the beach.

Breakfast is served each morning in the ocean-view dining room. Offerings, which incorporate organic products when possible, include vanilla pecan waffles, pumpkin ginger pancakes or blueberry cream cheese coffee cake.

INNKEEPERS:	Eric & Elaine Hillesland
ADDRESS:	44781 Main Street
	Mendocino, California 95460
TELEPHONE:	(707) 937-5150; (800) 780-7905
E-MAIL:	inn@oceanfrontmagic.com
WEBSITE:	www.oceanfrontmagic.com
ROOMS:	7 Rooms; Private baths
CHILDREN:	Welcome; Call ahead
ANIMALS:	Not allowed
HANDICAPPED:	Not handicapped accessible
DIETARY NEEDS:	Will accommodate guests' special dietary needs

Ginger Peach Pecan Scones

Makes 18 Scones

3½	cups all-purpose flour
¾	cup cornmeal
¾	cup sugar
2	tablespoons baking powder
½	teaspoon salt
1½	teaspoons nutmeg
1	teaspoon cinnamon
1	stick butter, cut into 16 (½-tablespoon) pieces
1¼	cups coarsely chopped fresh peaches, frozen for 1 hour
1	cup toasted pecans
¼	cup finely chopped candied ginger
⅔	cup half & half, plus extra for brushing on scones
4	large eggs
2	teaspoons vanilla extract

Vanilla sugar (sugar in which vanilla beans have been sitting)

Preheat oven to 425°F. In a food processor, combine flour, cornmeal, sugar, baking powder, salt, nutmeg and cinnamon; pulse to mix. Add butter pieces and pulse until cut in. Transfer mixture to a large bowl. Add peaches, pecans and candied ginger; stir just to combine.

In a medium bowl, combine half & half, eggs and vanilla; add to flour mixture and stir from bottom until a loose dough is formed.

Drop 18 large ice cream scoops of dough onto a large cookie sheet sprayed with non-stick cooking spray. Brush scones with half & half. Sprinkle with vanilla sugar. Bake for 15-17 minutes, or until golden brown.

J. Patrick House

Experience J. Patrick House, Cambria's original bed & breakfast inn, nestled in the tall Monterey pines above Cambria's charming east village. As you enter this enchanting log home, the warmth of its embrace welcomes you. The aroma of freshly baked cookies, homemade granola, breads and muffins will transport you to a magical place.

Discover numerous art galleries and antique and gift shops. Experience the beauty and tranquility of the countryside or walk along the shoreline and visit tide pools to watch the elephant seals, sea otters and whales.

INNKEEPERS:	Ann & John O'Connor
ADDRESS:	2990 Burton Drive
	Cambria, California 93428
TELEPHONE:	(805) 927-3812; (800) 341-5258
E-MAIL:	jph@jpatrickhouse.com
WEBSITE:	www.jpatrickhouse.com
ROOMS:	8 Rooms; Private baths
CHILDREN:	Children age 14 and older welcome
ANIMALS:	Not allowed; Resident dogs
HANDICAPPED:	Not handicapped accessible
DIETARY NEEDS:	Will accommodate guests' special dietary needs

JPH Cranberry Scones

Makes 16 Scones

½   cup dried cranberries
2   tablespoons brandy
1   teaspoon grated orange zest
4   cups all-purpose flour
¾   cup sugar
½   teaspoon salt
2   tablespoons baking powder
2   sticks unsalted butter or margarine
1¾ cups buttermilk, divided, plus more if needed

Preheat oven to 400°F. In a small bowl, combine cranberries, brandy and orange zest; microwave for 25 seconds. In a large bowl, combine flour, sugar, salt and baking powder. Cut in butter until there are no lumps larger than ¼-inch. Stir in cranberry mixture. Stir in 1 cup of buttermilk (if dough is crumbly, stir in more buttermilk until a smooth dough is formed).

Knead dough on a lightly floured surface until it holds together. Form dough into a ball and cut in half. Put dough on a cookie sheet and flatten each piece into a ½-inch-thick round. With a floured knife, cut each round in eighths. Brush each scone with 2 teaspoons of buttermilk. Bake for about 25-30 minutes, until golden brown. Transfer to wire rack to cool.

Capay Valley

Just a short drive from the Bay Area and Sacramento, the Capay Valley Bed & Breakfast sits peacefully surrounded by fountains and private sanctuaries. With over 70 animals on this 142 acre property, guests can take part in farm activities, adventures or just lounge by the pool.

Capay Valley offers the ultimate in casual relaxation. Play croquet, Bocci and horseshoes on the grassy lawn. Or head out on hiking and biking trails or a horseback ride – bike rentals and horse boarding are available.

INNKEEPERS:	Elizabeth Campbell
ADDRESS:	15875 State Highway 16
	Capay, California 95607
TELEPHONE:	(530) 796-3738; (866) 227-2922
E-MAIL:	campkebbb@afes.com
WEBSITE:	www.capayvalleybedandbreakfast.com
ROOMS:	4 Rooms; 2 Cottages; Private & shared baths
CHILDREN:	Call ahead
ANIMALS:	Call ahead
HANDICAPPED:	Handicapped accessible
DIETARY NEEDS:	Will accommodate guests' special dietary needs

World Famous Scones

Makes 10 to 12 Scones

"These scones are our signature dish. People just rave about them!" ~ Innkeeper, Capay Valley Bed & Breakfast

3	cups all-purpose flour
¼	teaspoon salt
⅓	cup white sugar
1½	sticks butter
2½	teaspoons baking powder
½	teaspoon baking soda

Grated zest and juice of 1 lemon
Grated zest of 1 orange

1	cup milk
¼	cup whipping cream
1	cup raisins or dried cherries or cranberries (or a mixture)
½	cup raw sugar
2	teaspoons cinnamon

Preheat oven to 450°F. In a food processor, pulse together flour, salt, white sugar, butter, baking powder, baking soda, lemon zest and orange zest.

In a small bowl, combine milk, cream and lemon juice; add to flour mixture in food processor. Add raisins and process until blended.

On a floured surface, roll dough out ⅓-inch thick. Cut dough with a medium or large biscuit cutter. Sprinkle with raw sugar and cinnamon. Bake on a greased cookie sheet for 15-18 minutes, or until golden brown.

China Creek

China Creek Bed & Breakfast is a unique contemporary estate with five acres of oaks and pines bordering China Creek. This site was home to Native Americans prior to the Gold Rush – arrowheads found on the property offer evidence of their lives. The inn is located in the heart of the village of Oakhurst and is 17 miles from Yosemite Park.

Visit Yosemite Park for the day, then return to the inn for a glass of sherry by the waterfall in the atrium or watch the sunset from the rose garden. Enjoy a hot breakfast each morning, then refresh yourself in the pool.

INNKEEPERS:	Peggy Stackhouse
ADDRESS:	49522 Road 426
	Oakhurst, California 93644
TELEPHONE:	(559) 642-6248; (888) 246-0720
E-MAIL:	chinacreek@webtv.net
WEBSITE:	chinacreekbedandbreakfast.com
ROOMS:	5 Rooms; Private & shared baths
CHILDREN:	Children age 12 and older welcome
ANIMALS:	Not allowed
HANDICAPPED:	Handicapped accessible
DIETARY NEEDS:	Will accommodate guests' special dietary needs

Hot & Crunchy Oatmeal

Makes 1 Serving

"This is a delicious oatmeal to warm your family or friends on a cold fall or winter morning. You will receive many compliments with this welcome addition to a healthy breakfast. Simply multiply the recipe for the needed number of servings." ~ Innkeeper, China Creek Bed & Breakfast

1   cup milk or water, plus extra warm milk, for serving
½   cup old-fashioned rolled oats
Dash of salt
1   teaspoon butter
1   tablespoon brown sugar
2   tablespoons chopped almonds, toasted

In a saucepan, bring milk or water to a boil. Add oats, salt, butter and brown sugar; stir together lightly and boil for 2 minutes. Cover pan, remove from heat and let stand for 4-5 minutes, or until water is absorbed (do not stir). Stir in chopped almonds. Serve with warm milk.

Tamarack Lodge at Bear Valley

The Tamarack Lodge at Bear Valley is a relaxed, casual inn located just six miles from Bear Valley Mountain Resort. This family-run and family-friendly bed & breakfast has rustic wood paneling and country decor, and is ideal for individuals, families or groups of up to 45 people.

Breakfast will prepare you for a day of outdoor activity. It consists of a variety of cereals, toast, bagels, muffins, fruit, juice, toaster waffles, the inn's special cinnamon pull-apart bread and a hot entrée such as scrambled eggs and cheese with hash browns and sausage.

INNKEEPERS:	Vicky and Tim Johnson
ADDRESS:	18278 Highway 4
	Tamarack-Bear Valley, California 95223
TELEPHONE:	(209) 753-2080; (877) 492-7013
E-MAIL:	innkeeper@tamarackholiday.com
WEBSITE:	www.tamarackholiday.com
ROOMS:	12 Rooms; 6 Suites; Private & shared baths
CHILDREN:	Welcome
ANIMALS:	Not allowed
HANDICAPPED:	Not handicapped accessible
DIETARY NEEDS:	Will accommodate guests' special dietary needs

Tamarack Muesli

Makes 16 Servings

"This recipe was created by innkeeper Vicky Johnson after living in Switzerland as program director for the International Girl Scout Outdoor Center. Muesli is eaten in Switzerland as an afternoon or evening snack. It is usually stirred into yogurt and fresh fruit and left to 'still' overnight in the refrigerator. This version is eaten at breakfast and can be served with fresh fruit and cold or hot milk or plain or fruit yogurt. It is filling and delicious – a great way to start a day of skiing, hiking or kayaking." – Innkeeper, Tamarack Lodge at Bear Valley

4	cups old-fashioned rolled oats
4	cups raisin bran or fruit bran cereal
1	cup chopped nuts (usually walnuts, though pecans are good, too)
¾	cup dried cranberries
¾	cup raisins
½	cup powdered sugar
½	cup powdered milk (optional)
1	heaping tablespoon cinnamon
½-1	cup dried fruit, such as banana chips or chopped apricots or apples (optional)

Milk or plain or fruit yogurt, for serving
Fresh fruit, such as blueberries, raspberries or sliced bananas or peaches, for serving (optional)

In a large bowl, combine oats and cereal. Add nuts, dried cranberries, and raisins. Stir in powdered sugar, powdered milk and cinnamon. Stir in dried fruit, if desired. Mix well and store in an air-tight container.

Serve ⅓-½ cup of muesli per person mixed with ½ cup of milk or ½ cup yogurt. Serve immediately or cover and refrigerate overnight to "still" (if soaking overnight, increase milk or yogurt to ¾ cup). Top with fresh fruit to serve, if desired.

Gerstle Park Inn

S et amongst the foothills, Gerstle Park Inn Bed & Breakfast is just minutes from San Francisco's Golden Gate Bridge, dramatic California coastline and myriad renowned Napa and Sonoma wineries. Guest rooms are named for flowers commonly found in England and include private decks and patios, down comforters, fine linens, a full gourmet breakfast and complimentary evening wine and snacks.

Stroll among heritage oaks and redwoods in neighboring Gerstle Park or relax on the veranda with iced tea and watch the day come to a close.

INNKEEPERS:	Jim Dowling
ADDRESS:	34 Grove Street
	San Rafael, California 94901
TELEPHONE:	(415) 721-7611; (800) 726-7611
E-MAIL:	innkeeper@gerstleparkinn.com
WEBSITE:	www.gerstleparkinn.com
ROOMS:	6 Rooms; 4 Suites; 2 Cottages; Private baths
CHILDREN:	Children age 12 and older welcome
ANIMALS:	Not allowed
HANDICAPPED:	Not handicapped accessible
DIETARY NEEDS:	Will accommodate guests' special dietary needs

Gerstle Park Inn Granola

Makes 20 Servings

Oat mixture:

8	cups old-fashioned rolled oats
¾	cup sliced raw almonds
¾	cup raw cashew halves
¾	cup raw sunflower seeds
1	cup dried coconut
½	cup dried date pieces
½	cup raisins or dried cranberries
2	teaspoons cinnamon

Liquid mixture:

½	cup canola oil
½	cup brown sugar
½	cup honey
½	cup maple syrup
¼	cup molasses
1	tablespoon vanilla extract
½	teaspoon salt

For the oat mixture: Preheat oven to 350°F. In a large bowl, combine oat mixture ingredients; divide oat mixture between 2 bowls.

For the liquid mixture: Spray a metal serving spoon and a baking sheet with non-stick cooking spray. In a glass bowl, combine all liquid mixture ingredients; heat in microwave until warm. Stir to combine, then pour equal amounts of liquid mixture over oat mixture in each bowl.

Spread ¼ of granola on each baking sheet. Bake, stirring every 5 minutes with metal spoon, until lightly browned throughout. Remove granola to a large bowl. Repeat with remaining granola. Store in an air-tight container.

French Toast, Bread Puddings, Pancakes & Waffles

French Toast, Bread Puddings, Pancakes & Waffles

Whitegate Inn

Step inside the Whitegate Inn and enjoy a sense of informal luxury. Decor is elegant, set off by striking antiques and fresh flowers. Cross the threshold into the drawing room where you can mingle with other guests or take in the ocean view. Rooms are generously appointed with fireplaces and irresistibly plush European feather beds.

"Perhaps the only way to coax visitors out of their comfy rooms in the morning is the aroma of the lavish breakfasts, which might include homemade scones or caramel-apple French toast." ~ *Bon Appétit*

INNKEEPERS:	Susan & Richard Strom
ADDRESS:	499 Howard Street
	Mendocino, California 95460
TELEPHONE:	(707) 937-4892; (800) 531-7282
E-MAIL:	staff@whitegateinn.com
WEBSITE:	www.whitegateinn.com
ROOMS:	6 Rooms; 1 Cottage; Private baths
CHILDREN:	Children age 10 and older welcome
ANIMALS:	Small dogs welcome in cottage; Resident dogs
HANDICAPPED:	Not handicapped accessible
DIETARY NEEDS:	Will accommodate guests' special dietary needs

Caramel Apple French Toast

Makes 6 Servings

"This is our signature breakfast dish. We serve it every Sunday morning with chicken-apple sausage and Thanksgiving coffee. Plan ahead – the French toast needs to be started the night before." ~ Innkeeper, Whitegate Inn

1	stick butter
1	cup brown sugar
3	tablespoons Karo syrup
1	cup chopped pecans
6	eggs
1½	cups milk
1	teaspoon vanilla extract
12	slices French bread (not sourdough)
9	large tart apples, peeled and thinly sliced

Cinnamon, to taste
Nutmeg, to taste
Maple syrup, for serving

Melt butter in a saucepan over medium heat. Stirring constantly, add brown sugar and Karo syrup. Just before syrup comes to a boil, pour into a greased 9x13-inch glass baking dish. Sprinkle with pecans.

In a bowl, beat eggs, milk and vanilla with a mixer until frothy. Dip 6 slices of bread in egg mixture and arrange on top of brown sugar mixture in baking dish. Top with apples (they should be piled high).

Dip remaining 6 slices of bread in egg mixture and align over bottom layer of bread atop apples. Pour remaining egg mixture over bread. Cover and refrigerate overnight.

The next day, preheat oven to 350°F. Sprinkle French toast with cinnamon and nutmeg. Bake for about 1 hour. Serve hot with warm maple syrup.

ON MIRAMAR BEACH

The Cypress Inn on Miramar Beach is an upscale bed & breakfast inn with outstanding, unobstructed ocean views and five miles of white sand beach. The goal of the inn's interior design is to bring the outdoors inside with a palette of nature's colors. Mexican folk art and hand-carved wooden animals add to the colorful celebration of nature.

The breakfast menu varies daily with fresh fruit, home baked croissants and delicious entrées such as artichoke quiche, Spanish egg sarape or the house specialty – peaches and cream French toast.

INNKEEPERS:	Kelly Barba
ADDRESS:	407 Mirada Road
	Half Moon Bay, California 94019
TELEPHONE:	(650) 726-6002; (800) 832-3224
E-MAIL:	reservations@cypressinn.com
WEBSITE:	www.cypressinn.com
ROOMS:	18 Rooms; Private baths
CHILDREN:	Welcome; Call ahead
ANIMALS:	Not allowed
HANDICAPPED:	Handicapped accessible
DIETARY NEEDS:	Will accommodate guests' special dietary needs

Peaches & Cream French Toast

Makes 6 Servings

Plan ahead – this French toast needs to be refrigerated overnight.

French toast:
7   large eggs
3   cups heavy cream or half & half
1¼   loaves French bread, cut into 12 (1½-inch-thick) slices
2   tablespoons butter
Powdered sugar, for garnish
Mint sprigs, for garnish
12   fresh peach slices, for garnish

Peach sauce:
⅓   (16-ounce) package frozen peaches, thawed
1   cup heavy cream
¾   cup sugar

Raspberry sauce:
1¼   cups raspberries
¾   cup sugar

For the French toast: Combine eggs and cream. Pour a small amount of egg mixture in a greased 9x13-inch baking pan. Put bread in a single layer in pan. Pour remaining egg mixture over bread; let stand for 5 minutes, then turn slices over. Cover and refrigerate overnight.

The next day, preheat oven to 350°F. Melt butter in a skillet over medium heat. Cook French toast until golden brown on both sides. Transfer to a baking sheet and bake for 5-7 minutes. Pour ¼ cup of peach sauce on each plate. Put 2 pieces of French toast on top of sauce. Dust with powdered sugar. Garnish with a mint sprig, 2 peach slices and a little raspberry sauce.

For the peach sauce: Blend peaches, cream and sugar until smooth.

For the raspberry sauce: Blend raspberries and sugar until smooth.

Joshua Grindle Inn

The AAA Four-Diamond Joshua Grindle Inn is a beautiful 19th-century ocean-view home, surrounded by two acres of lush gardens. The inn offers the leisure and solitude you seek, yet it is an easy walk to everything in the village of Mendocino. Guests can hike the coast, browse the shops in Mendocino, horseback ride on the beach, read in the inn's gardens or dine in one of Mendocino's award-winning restaurants.

Amenities include luxurious robes and fine toiletries, such as locally-made glycerin soaps, Mendocino Cookie Company cookies and Husch wines.

INNKEEPERS:	Charles & Cindy Reinhart
ADDRESS:	44800 Little Lake Road
	Mendocino, California 95460
TELEPHONE:	(707) 937-4143; (800) 474-6353
E-MAIL:	stay@joshgrin.com
WEBSITE:	www.joshgrin.com
ROOMS:	8 Rooms; 2 Cottages; Private baths
CHILDREN:	Children age 12 and older welcome
ANIMALS:	Not allowed; Resident cats
HANDICAPPED:	Handicapped accessible; Call ahead
DIETARY NEEDS:	Will accommodate guests' special dietary needs

Cranberry Pumpkin French Toast

Makes 12 Servings

Plan ahead – this French toast needs to be started the night before.

12	slices sourdough bread, cut into 1-inch cubes
1	(8-ounce) package cream cheese, cubed
1	(16-ounce) package fresh or frozen cranberries or 1 (16-ounce) can whole cranberries
12	large eggs
2	cups milk
2	cups canned pumpkin
1	tablespoon cinnamon
1	teaspoon ground cloves
1½	teaspoons ground ginger
1½	teaspoons nutmeg

Cranberry sauce:

1	(16-ounce) can jellied cranberry sauce
½	cup sugar, or to taste
½	cup water, about

Spray a 10x15-inch baking pan with non-stick cooking spray. Place ½ of bread cubes in bottom of pan. Top with cream cheese. Top cream cheese with ¾ of cranberries. Top with remaining bread and cranberries.

Beat together eggs, milk, pumpkin, cinnamon, cloves, ginger and nutmeg; pour over bread. Cover with plastic wrap and press firmly so bread soaks up egg mixture. Refrigerate overnight.

The next day, preheat oven to 350°F. Bake French toast for 40 minutes (check after 25 minutes – if French toast is browning too quickly, cover with foil). Let stand for 10 minutes. Slice and serve with cranberry sauce.

For the cranberry sauce: Heat cranberry sauce and sugar in a saucepan over medium-low heat. Cook, stirring, until sugar dissolves. Thin with water to desired consistency.

Candlelight Inn

B uilt in 1929 by the local postmaster, the Candlelight Inn is an exquisite example of English Tudor architecture. With whitewashed plaster set between blackened oak timbers, the inn reflects light both inside and out. This exceedingly romantic and soothing environment is perfect for a visit to the Wine Country. Secluded beneath towering redwoods along the banks of Napa Creek, the inn sits on an acre of quiet, park-like grounds.

A three-course, gourmet breakfast, wine and hors d'oeuvres, elegant guestrooms and luxurious amenities make your stay one to remember.

INNKEEPERS:	Mark & Wendy Tamiso
ADDRESS:	1045 Easum Drive
	Napa, California 94558
TELEPHONE:	(707) 257-3717; (800) 624-0395
E-MAIL:	mail@candlelightinn.com
WEBSITE:	www.candlelightinn.com
ROOMS:	10 Rooms; Private baths
CHILDREN:	Call ahead
ANIMALS:	Not allowed
HANDICAPPED:	Handicapped accessible
DIETARY NEEDS:	Will accommodate guests' special dietary needs

Croissant French Toast with Spiced Apples, Pears & Cranberries

Makes 12 Servings

Spiced apple, pear & cranberry topping:

1½	cups frozen cranberries
1	teaspoon plus 1 tablespoon Grand Marnier
¾	cup loosely packed brown sugar, divided
¾	stick butter
4	medium Fuji apples, peeled and diced
4	medium Granny Smith apples, peeled and diced
6	Bartlett pears, peeled and diced
2-3	tablespoons cinnamon
⅛	teaspoon nutmeg
½	cup maple syrup

French toast:

2	cups half & half or cream
4	large eggs
1	tablespoon cinnamon
¼	cup powdered sugar, plus extra for garnish
24	mini or 12 large croissants, cut in half lengthwise

For the spiced apple topping: Combine cranberries, 1 teaspoon of Grand Marnier and 2 tablespoons of brown sugar in a saucepan over medium heat. Cook until cranberries are tender; set aside. Melt butter in a saucepan over medium heat. Add apples, pears, remaining brown sugar, cinnamon and nutmeg; cook for 5 minutes. Add 1 tablespoon of Grand Marnier and maple syrup; cook, stirring often, until fruit is tender. Remove from heat and stir in cranberry mixture.

For the French toast: Combine half & half, eggs, cinnamon and powdered sugar. Dip croissants into egg mixture. Cook on a hot, greased griddle or skillet until golden brown on both sides. Top with spiced apple topping and drizzle with topping pan juices. Dust with powdered sugar and serve.

Vine Hill Inn

This award-winning, beautifully remodeled 1897 Victorian farmhouse is located in west Sonoma County. Nestled between vineyards and apple orchards in rural Sebastopol, this casual yet tasteful country inn is just one hour from San Francisco. Unwind in this idyllic country setting, where guests are pampered with delicious breakfasts, Egyptian cotton towels and glorious views from the decks and porches.

The inn's location is ideal for winery touring, exploring the Russian River or whale watching and swimming at nearby beaches.

INNKEEPERS:	Kathy Deichmann
ADDRESS:	3949 Vine Hill Road
	Sebastopol, California 95472
TELEPHONE:	(707) 823-8832
E-MAIL:	innkeeper@vine-hill-inn.com
WEBSITE:	www.vine-hill-inn.com
ROOMS:	4 Rooms; Private baths
CHILDREN:	Call ahead
ANIMALS:	Small dogs welcome; Resident cat
HANDICAPPED:	Not handicapped accessible
DIETARY NEEDS:	Will accommodate guests' special dietary needs

Strawberry Croissant French Toast

Makes 8 Servings

8	croissants, halved lengthwise
1	(8-ounce) package cream cheese, softened
2	cups sliced strawberries, plus extra for garnish
3	large eggs
1	cup milk
1	teaspoon cinnamon
½	cup sugar
1	teaspoon nutmeg
1	teaspoon almond extract

Spread croissant bottoms with cream cheese. Top with strawberries, then sandwich with croissant tops. In a deep dish, beat together eggs, milk, cinnamon, sugar, nutmeg and almond extract. Dip croissants in egg mixture and cook on a hot, buttered griddle or skillet until golden brown on both sides (be careful – croissants burn easily). Garnish with sliced strawberries to serve.

Note: This recipe can easily be halved – just use 2 eggs instead of 3.

Cinnamon Bear Inn

Cinnamon Bear Inn is a quaint bed & breakfast nestled in the mountains of Mammoth Lakes. Conveniently located in the heart of downtown Mammoth Lakes, the inn offers easy access to ski lift shuttles, restaurants and shopping. Year-round lodging offers a comfortable, homey atmosphere along with a full breakfast and afternoon hors d'oeuvres.

Each room is individually decorated in a New England Colonial style. Romantic, four-poster canopy beds are available in some rooms.

INNKEEPERS:	Russ & Mary Ann Harrison
ADDRESS:	113 Center Street
	Mammoth Lakes, California 93546
TELEPHONE:	(760) 934-2873; (800) 845-2873
E-MAIL:	cinnabear1@aol.com
WEBSITE:	www.cinnamonbearinn.com
ROOMS:	16 Rooms; 6 Suites; Private baths
CHILDREN:	Welcome
ANIMALS:	Not allowed
HANDICAPPED:	Handicapped accessible
DIETARY NEEDS:	Will accommodate guests' special dietary needs

Raspberry & Cream Cheese-Stuffed French Toast

Makes 12 Servings

½   (10-ounce) package frozen raspberries
1   (8-ounce) package cream cheese
12   eggs
4   cups milk
2   tablespoons vanilla extract
1½   teaspoons cinnamon
1   loaf bread, sliced (your favorite)
Butter, for serving (optional)
Powdered sugar, for garnish
Maple syrup, for serving

Put raspberries and cream cheese in a small bowl and microwave for about 2 minutes, until cream cheese mixture is soft enough to blend; stir to combine. In a wide dish, combine eggs, milk, vanilla and cinnamon. Spread about 1 tablespoon of cream cheese mixture on ½ of bread slices. Sandwich with remaining bread slices.

Dunk each sandwich into egg mixture, coating both sides, and cook in a hot, buttered skillet or griddle until golden brown on both sides. Butter sandwiches, if desired. Dust with powdered sugar. Serve with maple syrup.

Tamarack Pines Inn

The Tamarack Pines Inn, located at 7,000 feet in the Sierra Nevada Mountains, is a perfect getaway for the family, the outdoor enthusiast or the urban escapist. The inn is just five miles from Bear Valley Mountain Resort and Lake Alpine and provides easy access to water sports, mountain biking, hiking, sledding and downhill and cross-country skiing.

Breakfast is served buffet-style and an array of snacks are always available. For the younger set, there is a game room with toys, games, books and a video library.

INNKEEPERS:	Vicky & Tim Johnson
ADDRESS:	18326 Highway 4
	Tamarack-Bear Valley, California 95223
TELEPHONE:	(209) 753-2895; (800) 753-2895
E-MAIL:	innkeeper@tamarackpinesinn.com
WEBSITE:	www.tamarackpinesinn.com
ROOMS:	2 Rooms; 5 Suites; 1 Cottage; Private & shared baths
CHILDREN:	Children age 12 and older welcome
ANIMALS:	Not allowed
HANDICAPPED:	Not handicapped accessible
DIETARY NEEDS:	Will accommodate guests' special dietary needs

Melt in Your Mouth Eggnog Morning Toast

Makes 12 Servings

"If you like French toast, you'll love this baked version with eggnog that is sure to please." ~ Innkeeper, Tamarack Pines Inn

4	cups eggnog (or 2 cups of eggnog and 2 cups of milk)
6	eggs (use 8 eggs if using 2 cups of eggnog and 2 cups of milk)
1	cup maple syrup
½	teaspoon cinnamon and/or nutmeg
1	teaspoon vanilla extract
1	tablespoon grated orange zest
1½	loaves sourdough bread, diced
1	(8-ounce) package cream cheese, softened
2	cups fresh or frozen blueberries or raspberries, plus extra for garnish

Powdered sugar, sifted, for garnish
Mint leaves, for garnish

Preheat oven to 350°F. Beat together eggnog, eggs, maple syrup, cinnamon, vanilla and orange zest. Put about ¾ of diced bread in a large bowl or baking pan. Add eggnog mixture and let bread soak for 20-30 minutes.

Layer unsoaked diced bread in a greased 9x13-inch baking dish. Spread cream cheese over bread. Sprinkle with berries. Spread soaked bread over berries. Bake for 50 minutes. Sprinkle with powdered sugar. Garnish with blueberries or raspberries and a mint leaf.

Churchill Manor

Churchill Manor is a magnificent, three-story, circa 1889 mansion listed on the National Register of Historic Places. Encompassing nearly 10,000-square-feet, it is reputed to be the largest home of its time built in Napa Valley. This storybook mansion is the legacy of businessman Edward S. Churchill, one of Napa's founders.

The mansion rests amid a private acre of mature trees, lush gardens, colorful tree roses, verdant, manicured lawns and a formal fountain. An expansive veranda surrounds three sides of this elegant mansion.

INNKEEPERS:	Joanna Guidotti & Brian Jensen
ADDRESS:	485 Brown Street
	Napa, California 94559
TELEPHONE:	(707) 253-7733; (800) 799-7733
E-MAIL:	be@churchillmanor.com
WEBSITE:	www.churchillmanor.com
ROOMS:	10 Rooms; Private baths
CHILDREN:	Children age 12 and older welcome
ANIMALS:	Not allowed; Resident cat
HANDICAPPED:	Handicapped accessible
DIETARY NEEDS:	Will accommodate guests' special dietary needs

Orange-Zested French Toast

"When you catch a sophisticated guest licking their plate, you know you are either a poor judge of character, or you have a winning breakfast entrée." ~ Innkeeper, Churchill Manor Bed & Breakfast

12	large eggs, beaten

Grated zest of 2 oranges

2	oranges (enough to yield 16 sections)
1	cup sour cream
2	tablespoons honey, warmed slightly (aids mixing)
2	tablespoons brandy
1-2	sourdough baguettes (enough to yield ¾-inch-thick 24 slices)
2	tablespoons butter, softened
2	cups pure maple syrup

Cinnamon, for garnish

Preheat oven to 350°F. Put beaten eggs in a shallow dish. Add orange zest and mix well. Peel oranges and remove orange sections to a plate or bowl.

Put sour cream in a small bowl. Add honey and brandy; stir to combine. Adjust taste as desired (it should be thick enough not to run). Cut baguette on the bias into ¾-inch-thick slices. Soak bread slices in egg mixture until well coated. Melt butter in a large skillet over medium-high heat. Cook French toast until browned on both sides.

Place 3 pieces of French toast on each plate, stacked in the middle and radiating outward like spokes on a wheel. Add a large dollop of the sour cream mixture to plate between one of the "spokes." Put 1 orange section in each of remaining 2 spaces between the "spokes." Top with maple syrup and a dusting of cinnamon.

Grand View Inn

The first female mayor of Pacific Grove, Julia Platt, built this remarkable home at the edge of Monterey Bay, that is now the Grand View Inn. The home retains all of the history, elegance, comfort and beauty with which it was constructed.

A feeling of quiet elegance encompasses the inn. Along with unsurpassed views of Monterey Bay from each room, guests enjoy the comfort of marble tiled baths, patterned hardwood floors, beautiful antique furnishings and lovely grounds.

INNKEEPERS:	Susan Wheelwright & Ed Flatley
ADDRESS:	557 Ocean View Boulevard
	Pacific Grove, California 93950
TELEPHONE:	(831) 372-4341
E-MAIL:	None available
WEBSITE:	www.pginns.com
ROOMS:	11 Rooms; 1 Suite; 1 Cottage; Private baths
CHILDREN:	Children age 12 and older welcome
ANIMALS:	Not allowed
HANDICAPPED:	Handicapped accessible
DIETARY NEEDS:	Will accommodate guests' special dietary needs

Pumpkin Bread Pudding

Makes 8 Servings

"The use of croissants instead of bread results in an ethereally light pudding. A very easy and versatile recipe – the pumpkin pie spices make this a wonderful autumnal dish." – Innkeeper, Grand View Inn

4½	cups large croissant cubes
6	large eggs
4	egg yolks
1	cup packed brown sugar, divided
2	teaspoons cinnamon
2	teaspoons ground cloves
2	teaspoons ground ginger
2	teaspoons nutmeg

Pinch of salt

2	teaspoons vanilla extract
1	(15-ounce) can pumpkin
2	cups milk
2	cups heavy cream
½	cup pecan halves

Whipped cream, for serving

Preheat oven to 350°F. Spread croissant cubes in a 9x13-inch baking dish sprayed with non-stick cooking spray. Beat eggs and egg yolks with a mixer at low speed until well mixed (or mix by hand). Add ½ cup of brown sugar, cinnamon, cloves, ginger, nutmeg, salt and vanilla, mix well. Add pumpkin; mix well. Add milk and cream; mix well.

Pour egg mixture over croissant cubes; stir briefly until croissant are well moistened. Sprinkle with remaining ½ cup of brown sugar and pecans. Bake bread pudding for about 45 minutes, until custard is set and top is golden brown. Serve hot or at room temperature with whipped cream.

The Brewery Gulch Inn

The Brewery Gulch Inn, built with ancient virgin redwood timbers eco-salvaged from Big River, sits on ten acres overlooking Smuggler's Cove. The inn, with its Craftsman-style architecture and décor, offers ocean views, fireplaces, Jacuzzi tubs, private decks, luxurious amenities, gourmet organic cuisine and comfortable, well-appointed rooms.

"From the moment we arrived to the moment we left, we felt wonderfully cared for. The accommodations were lovely and the food was comparable to a high-end restaurant." ~ *San Francisco Chronicle Sunday Travel*

INNKEEPERS:	Mina Lev & Patty Neumier
ADDRESS:	9401 Coast Highway One North
	Mendocino, California 95460
TELEPHONE:	(707) 937-4752; (800) 578-4454
E-MAIL:	info@brewerygulchinn.com
WEBSITE:	www.brewerygulchinn.com
ROOMS:	10 Rooms; Private baths
CHILDREN:	Children age 12 and older welcome
ANIMALS:	Not allowed
HANDICAPPED:	Handicapped accessible; 1 room
DIETARY NEEDS:	Will accommodate guests' special dietary needs

Chocolate Bread Pudding

Makes 8 to 10 Servings

"This is a great way to use up old croissants. Plan ahead – the bread pudding needs to be refrigerated for at least eight hours." ~ Innkeeper, Brewery Gulch Inn

1	teaspoon plus 1 cup sugar
¼	cup ricotta cheese or cream cheese
10	large croissants, torn into ½-inch pieces
½	cup chopped walnuts, toasted
¼	cup dried cherries
¼	cup semi-sweet chocolate chips
¼	cup unsweetened cocoa powder (Scharffen Berger is best), plus extra for dusting pan
¼	cup Kirsch (German cherry brandy)
12	eggs
1	cup heavy cream

Combine ricotta cheese with 1 teaspoon of sugar. In a bowl, toss together croissant pieces, walnuts, dried cherries, chocolate chips, ricotta mixture and cocoa powder. Add Kirsch and stir just to lightly combine. Butter a Bundt pan and dust lightly with cocoa. Put croissant mixture in pan. Combine eggs, cream and 1 cup of sugar; pour over croissant mixture. Cover tightly and refrigerate for at least 8 hours or overnight.

About an hour before baking, remove bread pudding from refrigerator and let it come to room temperature. Preheat oven to 350°F. Bake bread pudding for 15 minutes. Rotate pan 180° and bake for 15 minutes longer, until center is set and a toothpick inserted in center comes out clean.

Olallieberry Inn

Olallieberry Inn

The Olallieberry Inn is a historic bed & breakfast located in the seaside village of Cambria on California's central coast. The home, built in 1863, sits on Santa Rosa Creek. A 120-year-old redwood tree greets guests, and lush, colorful gardens can be enjoyed from the back deck.

In the afternoon, enjoy complimentary local wine and sumptuous hors d'oeuvres, such as baked Brie in puff pastry with toasted almonds, goat cheese and roasted garlic with freshly baked focaccia or crab pâté. And, of course, there is an endless supply of home-baked cookies.

INNKEEPERS:	Marjorie Ott and Marilyn & Larry Draper
ADDRESS:	2476 Main Street
	Cambria, California 93428
TELEPHONE:	(805) 927-3222; (888) 927-3222
E-MAIL:	info@olallieberry.com
WEBSITE:	www.olallieberry.com
ROOMS:	9 Rooms; 1 Suites; Private baths
CHILDREN:	Welcome
ANIMALS:	Not allowed
HANDICAPPED:	Handicapped accessible
DIETARY NEEDS:	Will accommodate guests' special dietary needs

Orange & Cranberry Soufflé

Makes 10 Servings

"This is a favorite among our guests. Plan ahead – the soufflé needs to be refrigerated overnight." - Innkeeper, Olallieberry Inn

1	(8-ounce) package cream cheese, softened
1	stick butter, softened
½	cup maple syrup
¼	cup orange juice

Grated zest of 1 orange

8	large croissants
8	large eggs
2	cups half & half
¾	cup dried cranberries
1	teaspoon cinnamon

Powdered sugar, for garnish

Break up croissants into large pieces and scatter into a greased 9x13-inch baking dish. Combine cream cheese, butter, maple syrup, orange juice and orange zest until well mixed. Using a spatula, gently spread cream cheese mixture over croissants.

Beat eggs, half & half, cranberries and cinnamon; pour over ingredients in baking dish. Cover and refrigerate overnight.

The next day, preheat oven to 350°F. Remove soufflé from refrigerator, uncover and let come to room temperature. Bake for 45 minutes, or until golden brown. Dust with powdered sugar to serve.

Shooting Star

Escape to the Shooting Star Bed & Breakfast on the magnificent North Shore of Lake Tahoe. Revel in the natural beauty of Carnelian Bay, then retire to the warmth and comfort of the inn's casually elegant rooms. Wake to exceptional food and the endless possibilities of a day in Lake Tahoe – skiing, biking, boating, golfing, fishing – whatever stirs your soul!

Savor a delicious breakfast on your own time and at your own pace. The inn offers homemade fare from original recipes, such as banana bread pancakes and eggs Lulu, full-roasted coffee and fresh fruit and juice.

INNKEEPERS:	Marjorie Woodbridge
ADDRESS:	315 Olive Street
	Carnelian Bay, Lake Tahoe, California 96140
TELEPHONE:	(530) 546-8903; (888) 985-7827
E-MAIL:	innkeeper@shootingstarbandb.com
WEBSITE:	shootingstarbandb.com
ROOMS:	3 Rooms; 1 Suite; Private baths
CHILDREN:	Children age 12 and older welcome
ANIMALS:	Not allowed
HANDICAPPED:	Handicapped accessible
DIETARY NEEDS:	Will accommodate guests' special dietary needs

Banana Bread Pancakes

Makes 4 Servings

1½   cups all-purpose flour
1   teaspoon salt
3   tablespoons sugar
1   teaspoon cinnamon
1¾   teaspoons baking powder
½   teaspoon nutmeg
½   teaspoon ground ginger
2   eggs, separated
3   tablespoons butter, melted
1¼   cups milk
1   teaspoon vanilla extract
2   bananas, sliced
½   cup chopped walnuts
Applesauce, warmed, for serving

Caramelized bananas:
3   tablespoons butter
2   tablespoons packed brown sugar
2   tablespoons white sugar
½   teaspoon nutmeg
3   bananas, sliced on a slight diagonal

For the pancakes: In a large bowl, combine flour, salt, sugar, cinnamon, baking powder, nutmeg and ginger. In a medium bowl, combine egg yolks, butter, milk and vanilla; add to flour mixture and mix briefly (batter will be lumpy). Beat egg whites until stiff peaks form; gently fold into batter. Gently fold in bananas and walnuts (reserve 1 tablespoon of walnuts for garnish). Cook pancakes until golden brown on both sides. Top with caramelized bananas and reserved walnuts. Serve with warm applesauce.

For the bananas: Melt butter in a non-stick saucepan over medium heat. Add brown and white sugar and nutmeg; cook until sugars dissolve. Add bananas; cook until mixture thickens and bananas start to brown. (Optional: add 2 tablespoons of Kahlúa and cook for 3-5 minutes longer, until thickened.)

Inn on Randolph

The Inn on Randolph consists of four buildings, a Gothic Revival Victorian built in 1860 and three cottages added in the 1930s – all have been restored and individually furnished with loving care. Situated on a half-acre of landscaped lawn and gardens in quiet "Old Town" Napa, the property is within walking distance of downtown shops, restaurants and attractions such as Copia and the Napa Wine Train.

Relax in the parlor with a glass of premium wine, gather around the grand piano for an impromptu sing-along or swing in the garden hammock.

INNKEEPERS:	Deborah Coffee
ADDRESS:	411 Randolph Street
	Napa, California 94559
TELEPHONE:	(707)257-2886; (800) 670-6886
E-MAIL:	innonrandolph@aol.com
WEBSITE:	www.innonrandolph.com
ROOMS:	5 Rooms; 4 Suites; 3 Cottages; Private baths
CHILDREN:	Welcome
ANIMALS:	Not allowed; Resident cat
HANDICAPPED:	Handicapped accessible
DIETARY NEEDS:	Will accommodate guests' special dietary needs

Spicy Apple Gingerbread Pancakes

Makes 4 Servings

"These pancakes are a favorite all year but are especially popular during cooler fall and winter months." - Innkeeper, Inn on Randolph

3	large eggs
¼	cup packed light brown sugar
2	cups buttermilk
½	stick butter, melted and cooled
2½	cups all-purpose flour
1	teaspoon baking soda
1	tablespoon cinnamon
1	tablespoon nutmeg
1	teaspoon ground cloves
1	teaspoon ground ginger

Spicy apples:

4	Granny Smith or Golden Delicious apples, peeled and cut into ¼-inch-thick slices or small cubes
½	teaspoon cinnamon
½	teaspoon nutmeg
¼	teaspoon ground cloves
¼	cup packed light brown sugar
¼	cup apple juice or apple cider
½	stick butter, melted

In a medium bowl, combine eggs and brown sugar. Stir in buttermilk and butter. Sift together flour, baking soda, cinnamon, nutmeg, cloves and ginger into a large bowl. Stir egg mixture into flour mixture (do not overmix). Add more buttermilk, if needed (batter should be thick). Cook pancakes on a preheated, greased griddle or skillet until golden brown on both sides. Serve pancakes topped with spicy apples.

For the apples: In a small saucepan over low heat, combine all ingredients. Cook, stirring frequently, until apples are tender, but not mushy.

Case Ranch Inn

The Case Ranch Inn is a peaceful respite in a quiet country location, where guests rave about the unparalleled hospitality and graciousness of the hosts. Enjoy antique shopping in Sebastopol and Healdsburg, hike in beautiful Armstrong Woods State Park, taste award-winning wines at nearby Sonoma County wineries or visit the magnificent coastline where the Russian River meets the sea.

In the evening, enjoy the warm surroundings of the large parlor with its fireplace and comfortable wicker furniture.

INNKEEPERS:	Diana Van Ry & Allan Tilton
ADDRESS:	7446 Poplar Drive
	Forestville, California, 95436
TELEPHONE:	(707) 887-8711
E-MAIL:	info@caseranchinn.com
WEBSITE:	www.caseranchinn.com
ROOMS:	3 Rooms; 1 Cottage; Private baths
CHILDREN:	Children age 10 and older welcome
ANIMALS:	Not allowed
HANDICAPPED:	Not handicapped accessible
DIETARY NEEDS:	Will accommodate guests' special dietary needs

Lemon Oat Bran Pancakes

Makes 6 Servings

"You can easily turn these into blueberry lemon oat bran pancakes by simply stirring one cup of blueberries into the batter." ~ Innkeeper, Case Ranch Inn

1½	cups all-purpose flour
½	cup oat bran
1	tablespoon sugar
2	teaspoons baking powder
1	teaspoon baking soda
½	teaspoon salt, or to taste
2	large eggs
3	tablespoons butter, melted, or vegetable oil
2	tablespoons lemon juice
2	teaspoons grated lemon zest
1¾	cups milk
1	cup blueberries (optional)

In a large bowl, combine flour, oat bran, sugar, baking powder, baking soda and salt. In a medium bowl, beat eggs. Mix butter, lemon juice and lemon zest into eggs. Mix in milk. Add egg mixture to flour mixture; stir until fairly smooth. Stir in blueberries, if desired. Let batter stand for 5 minutes.

Heat a skillet or griddle over medium-high heat until a drop of water dances across surface of pan before evaporating (if you are not using a non-stick skillet or griddle, brush surface lightly with butter or oil). Add batter by ¼-cupsful to skillet. Cook pancakes until golden brown on each side.

Ten Inverness Way

Ten Inverness Way Bed & Breakfast is located off the breathtaking Marin Coast in the heart of Point Reyes National Seashore, steps from Tomales Bay and near the towns of Olema, Inverness Park and Point Reyes Station. The 1904 Craftsman inn is surrounded by lush gardens, filled with the aroma of home baking and appointed with the finest decor.

"We have found a cottage-away-from-home in the sleepy, lush, waterfront village of Inverness. Curl up in the main room in front of the stone fireplace and settle in for a weekend of serenity." ~ *San Francisco Examiner*

INNKEEPERS:	Teri Mattson
ADDRESS:	10 Inverness Way
	Inverness, California 94937
TELEPHONE:	(415) 669-1648
E-MAIL:	inn@teninvernessway.com
WEBSITE:	www.teninvernessway.com
ROOMS:	5 Rooms; Private baths
CHILDREN:	Children age 12 and older welcome
ANIMALS:	Not allowed
HANDICAPPED:	Handicapped accessible; 1 room
DIETARY NEEDS:	Will accommodate guests' special dietary needs

Banana Buttermilk Pancakes

Makes 8 Servings

"We serve these pancakes with chicken-apple sausage and maple syrup." ~
Innkeeper, Ten Inverness Way

4	eggs
2	cups all-purpose flour
2	cups whole-wheat flour
4	cups buttermilk
½	cup vegetable oil
¼	cup sugar
4	teaspoons baking powder
2	teaspoons baking soda
2	teaspoons salt
1	teaspoon nutmeg
4	ripe bananas, mashed

Orange slices, for garnish
Mint sprigs, for garnish
Powdered sugar, for garnish
Butter, for serving
Maple syrup, for serving

Preheat oven to 350°F. Beat together all ingredients, except garnish and serving ingredients, until smooth and fluffy (the more air in the batter the lighter the pancakes). Pour batter by ¼-cupful onto a preheated, greased griddle or skillet. Cook until lightly browned on both sides. Garnish with orange slices and a mint sprig. Dust with powdered sugar. Serve with butter and maple syrup.

Thistle Dew Inn

The Thistle Dew Inn Bed & Breakfast is located in the charming town of Sonoma, one of the state's most historic communities. The inn's superb location in a residential area, just one-half block from the Sonoma Plaza makes for easy walking to the area's many restaurants, shops and historic sites. Sonoma's premium wineries are just a short bike ride away.

The Arts & Crafts Movement embodied principles of quality, value, beauty and simplicity. The Thistle Dew Inn reflects those ideals and, accordingly, provides exceptional lodging that is restful, tasteful and warm.

INNKEEPERS:	Jan Rafiq & Gregg Percival
ADDRESS:	171 West Spain Street
	Sonoma, California 95476
TELEPHONE:	(707) 938-2909; (800) 382-7895
E-MAIL:	info@thistledew.com
WEBSITE:	www.thistledew.com
ROOMS:	5 Rooms; 1 Suite; Private baths
CHILDREN:	Children age 12 and older welcome
ANIMALS:	Not allowed; Resident cat
HANDICAPPED:	Handicapped accessible
DIETARY NEEDS:	Will accommodate guests' special dietary needs

Lemon Poppy Seed Pancakes with Honey Butter

Makes 8 to 10 Servings

Pancakes:

3	cups unbleached all-purpose flour
1	cup quick-cooking oats
¼	cup baking powder
1	teaspoon baking soda
½	teaspoon salt
5	eggs, lightly beaten
1	cup sour cream
1½	cups milk
1½	cups water

Grated zest of 2 lemons

1	teaspoon lemon oil
¼	cup poppy seeds
½	teaspoon vanilla powder or extract

Honey butter:

1	stick butter
½	cup honey

For the pancakes: Combine flour, oats, baking powder, baking soda and salt. Add eggs, sour cream, milk and water; beat just until blended, but still lumpy. Add lemon zest, lemon oil, poppy seeds and vanilla powder or extract; mix thoroughly. Let batter stand for 30 minutes (or cover and refrigerate overnight). Add more milk or water, if needed. Spoon batter onto a hot, buttered griddle or skillet and cook pancakes until browned on both sides. Serve with honey butter.

For the honey butter: Melt butter in a saucepan over low heat. Slowly add honey, stirring constantly, until smooth and opaque. Remove from heat and cool slightly.

Blue Spruce Inn

Affordable luxury combined with uncompromising personal service distinguishes the Blue Spruce Inn. The inn is 40 minutes from Carmel and Monterey, four miles from Santa Cruz and just a mile to the beaches of Capitola-by-the-Sea. In earlier times, Soquel was home to Native Americans who gave the village its name, which means "place of the willows."

Breakfast begins with seasonal fresh fruit from local growers followed by home baked cinnamon rolls, muffins or croissants. Entrées might include peach vanilla French toast, gingerbread waffles or eggs with fresh herb.

INNKEEPERS:	Nancy, Wayne & Carissa Lussier
ADDRESS:	2815 South Main Street
	Soquel, California 95073
TELEPHONE:	(831) 464-1137; (800) 559-1137
E-MAIL:	info@bluespruce.com
WEBSITE:	www.bluespruce.com
ROOMS:	6 Rooms; Private baths
CHILDREN:	Children age 13 and older welcome
ANIMALS:	Not allowed
HANDICAPPED:	Not handicapped accessible
DIETARY NEEDS:	Will accommodate guests' special dietary needs

Gingerbread Waffles

Makes 4 to 6 Waffles

"This is one of our big crowd pleasers." ~ Innkeeper, Blue Spruce Inn

2	cups all-purpose flour
½	teaspoon salt
1	teaspoon baking powder
1	teaspoon ground ginger
1	teaspoon cinnamon
¼	teaspoon ground cloves
1	cup molasses, warmed slightly (aids mixing)
1	cup milk
1	egg, beaten
½	cup vegetable oil

Sweetened whipped cream, for serving
Lemon curd, for serving
Maple syrup, for serving

In a large bowl, combine flour, salt, baking powder, ginger, cinnamon and cloves. In a medium bowl, combine molasses, milk, egg and oil. Add egg mixture to flour mixture; stir until well combined (add a little more milk, if needed). Bake in a preheated, non-stick or greased waffle iron until golden brown. Serve with whipped cream, lemon curd and maple syrup.

Carter House Inns

With perfect grace, the Carter House Inns unite contemporary good taste with the gracious elegance of a bygone era. Large windows invite streams of sunlight into the inn's four mansions, where rich fabrics, original local art and fresh flowers splash vibrant color in every room.

Rooms feature antique appointments and luxurious amenities suitable for even the most indulgent hedonist. Marble fireplaces, whirlpool baths with marina vistas, immense four-poster beds and double-headed showers hint at the pleasures that await you.

INNKEEPERS:	Mark & Christi Carter
ADDRESS:	301 L Street
	Eureka, California 95501
TELEPHONE:	(707) 444-8062
E-MAIL:	reserve@carterhouse.com
WEBSITE:	www.carterhouse.com
ROOMS:	22 Rooms; 8 Suites; 2 Cottages; Private baths
CHILDREN:	Welcome
ANIMALS:	Not allowed
HANDICAPPED:	Handicapped accessible
DIETARY NEEDS:	Will accommodate guests' special dietary needs

Fresh Corn Waffles with Cilantro Butter

Makes 3 to 4 Servings

"Like no other waffles you have had before." ~ Innkeeper, Carter House Inns

1	cup all-purpose flour
½	cup yellow cornmeal
2	tablespoons sugar
2	teaspoons baking powder
¼	teaspoon salt
1	large egg
2	tablespoons unsalted butter, melted and cooled
½	cup water
1	cup fresh corn
1	teaspoon vanilla extract

Maple syrup, for serving

Cilantro butter:

½	stick unsalted butter, softened
¼	cup chopped cilantro

In a large bowl, combine flour, cornmeal, sugar, baking powder and salt. In a medium bowl, whisk together egg, butter, water, corn and vanilla. Add egg mixture to flour mixture; mix just until combined. Bake waffles on a preheated, greased or non-stick waffle iron until golden. Top each waffle with cilantro butter and serve with maple syrup.

For the cilantro butter: Whisk together butter and cilantro until smooth and creamy.

Egg Dishes & Breakfast Entrées

Egg Dishes
&
Breakfast Entrées

The Inn at Occidental

Minutes from Sonoma Wine Country, the stunning Pacific coast and the charming Russian River, the Inn at Occidental offers a luxury inn experience that will lure you back again and again. Expect a warm welcome from the owners and the gracious staff. Mention an interest, and you'll soon have a customized map and list of activities in your hands. In the afternoon, a selection of hors d'oeuvres and local wines await you.

"The inn spoils guests with fireplaces, spa tubs and the world's best granola." ~ *Via Magazine*

INNKEEPERS:	Jerry & Tina Wolsborn
ADDRESS:	3657 Church Street
	Occidental, California 95465
TELEPHONE:	(707) 874-1047; (800) 522-6324
E-MAIL:	innkeeper@innatoccidental.com
WEBSITE:	www.innatoccidental.com
ROOMS:	15 Rooms; 3 Suites; 1 Cottage; Private baths
CHILDREN:	Children age 12 and older welcome
ANIMALS:	Small dogs in cottage only; Resident dogs
HANDICAPPED:	Handicapped accessible
DIETARY NEEDS:	Will accommodate guests' special dietary needs

Corn Fritters with Poached Eggs, Smoked Salmon & Crème Fraîche

Makes 6 Servings

1	cup boiling water
1	cup yellow or white cornmeal
½	stick butter
9	eggs, divided
1	cup milk
1	cup all-purpose flour
1½	teaspoons baking powder
3	tablespoons sugar
¼	cup diced red bell pepper
1½	cups fresh corn
¼	cup chopped green onion
12	slices smoked salmon
½	cup crème fraîche or sour cream, for serving
¼	cup minced red onion, for garnish
¼	cup finely chopped parsley, for garnish

In a large bowl, combine boiling water, cornmeal and butter; cool, then stir to form a smooth paste.

In a small bowl, beat together 3 eggs and milk; add to cornmeal mixture and mix until smooth. In a medium bowl, combine flour, baking powder and sugar; add to cornmeal mixture and mix until combined. Fold in red bell pepper, corn and green onions. Cook fritters in a greased skillet over medium heat until browned on both sides, making 12 fritters.

Poach remaining 6 eggs. Arrange 2 fritters on each plate. Top each serving with 2 slices of smoked salmon and 1 poached egg. Top with a dollop of crème fraîche. Sprinkle with red onion and parsley to serve.

Seven Gables Inn

Completed in 1886, the Seven Gables Inn is one of a parade of showy Victorians built along the oceanfront of the Monterey Peninsula. Today, guests can gaze out beveled windows at an unobstructed view of the Monterey Bay and the coastal mountains beyond.

Colorful gardens surround the inn, and guests will encounter a profusion of blooming flowers year-round. Breakfast, a lavish and elegant affair, is served in the main dining room. The lovely ritual of afternoon tea features delicious, homemade treats and imported cakes.

INNKEEPERS:	Susan Wheelwright & Ed Flatley
ADDRESS:	555 Ocean View Boulevard
	Pacific Grove, California 93950
TELEPHONE:	(831) 372-4341
E-MAIL:	None available
WEBSITE:	www.pginns.com
ROOMS:	14 Rooms; 1 Suite; 3 Cottages; Private baths
CHILDREN:	Children age 12 and older welcome
ANIMALS:	Not allowed
HANDICAPPED:	Handicapped accessible
DIETARY NEEDS:	Will accommodate guests' special dietary needs

Asparagus with Poached Eggs & Pancetta

Makes 8 Servings

"This was inspired by a traditional Italian recipe. It works beautifully as an elegant breakfast dish." - Innkeeper, Seven Gables Inn

Lime beurre blanc sauce:

1	shallot, minced
2	tablespoons seasoned rice wine vinegar
½	teaspoon ground coriander
½	teaspoon sugar
½	cup white wine or Champagne

Juice and grated zest of 1 lime

2	tablespoons butter, cut into 3 pieces

Salt & white pepper, to taste

Asparagus with poached eggs:

2	bunches asparagus, ends trimmed
8	large eggs, poached soft
6	slices pancetta, cut into matchstick strips
½	cup shaved Parmesan cheese

Freshly ground pepper, to taste
Freshly grated nutmeg, to taste

For the sauce: Heat a heavy skillet over medium heat. Combine shallots, vinegar, coriander and sugar; add to skillet. Add wine and cook, whisking occasionally, until shallots are very tender and liquid is reduced by half. Whisk in lime juice and zest. Add butter, 1 piece at a time piece, whisking well after each addition until combined. Season with salt and white pepper.

For the asparagus and poached egg: Preheat oven to 400°F. Put asparagus in a baking dish. Scatter pancetta over asparagus. Bake until asparagus is just tender and pancetta has begun to crisp. Remove from oven and divide among plates. Top with a poached egg. Sprinkle with Parmesan cheese. Drizzle with beurre blanc sauce. Season with pepper and nutmeg.

Ridenhour Ranch House Inn

Built along the Russian River, near the town of Guerneville, the circa 1906 Ridenhour Ranch House Inn has a history and charm all its own. Little more than an hour north of San Francisco, the inn is conveniently located near wineries, critically acclaimed restaurants, recreational activities and all that Sonoma County has to offer.

Guest rooms are decorated with a pleasing mix of antiques and country casual furnishings. All rooms include fresh flowers, Ghiradelli chocolates and fluffy terry cloth robes.

INNKEEPERS:	Chris Bell & Meilani Naranjo
ADDRESS:	12850 River Road
	Guerneville, California 95446
TELEPHONE:	(707) 887-1033; (888) 877-4466
E-MAIL:	innkeeper@ridenhourranchhouseinn.com
WEBSITE:	www.ridenhourranchhouseinn.com
ROOMS:	8 Rooms; 1 Suite; 1 Cottage; Private baths
CHILDREN:	Welcome
ANIMALS:	Dogs welcome in cottage
HANDICAPPED:	Handicapped accessible
DIETARY NEEDS:	Will accommodate guests' special dietary needs

Mini Soufflés

Makes 4 Servings

½   cup grated cheese (Gruyère or Swiss are good)
½   cup diced ham
4   mushrooms, thinly sliced
Nutmeg
4   eggs
1   cup heavy cream

Preheat oven to 350°F. Butter 4 individual-size ramekins and place them on a baking sheet. Sprinkle grated cheese over bottoms of ramekins. Divide ham and mushrooms among ramekins. Top with a pinch of nutmeg.

Whisk eggs well. Slowly whisk in heavy cream. Divide egg mixture among ramekins. Bake for about 30 minutes, or until soufflés are puffed and golden (soufflés can be held in a warm oven for about 20 minutes before they begin to deflate).

The Honor Mansion

B reakfasts at the Honor Mansion are a culinary treat. Two to three courses are served on the inn's antique china, silver and crystal. Weather permitting, the tables on the koi pond deck will be set so guests can enjoy breakfast with the sounds of the waterfall and the warmth of the morning sun glistening through the redwood trees surrounding the pond.

"Once in a while we stumble across a place that is so close to flawless it quickly reminds us why we do what we do. The Honor Mansion is one of those places." ~ *Best Places to Kiss in Northern California*

INNKEEPERS:	Steve & Cathi Fowler
ADDRESS:	14891 Grove Street
	Healdsburg, California 95448
TELEPHONE:	(707) 433-4277; (800) 554-4667
E-MAIL:	innkeeper@honormansion.com
WEBSITE:	www.honormansion.com
ROOMS:	5 Rooms; 7 Suites; 2 Cottages; Private baths
CHILDREN:	Not allowed
ANIMALS:	Not allowed
HANDICAPPED:	Handicapped accessible; 1 room
DIETARY NEEDS:	Will accommodate guests' special dietary needs

Mexican Soufflé with Ham

Makes 8 Servings

1   (4-ounce) can chopped mild green chilies
1   cup grated cheddar or Monterey Jack cheese
1   cup chopped ham
8   eggs
2   cups heavy cream
Salt and pepper, to taste
Guacamole, salsa, sour cream and sliced or chopped tomatoes, for serving

Preheat oven to 350°F. Generously spray 8 individual-size ramekins with non-stick cooking spray. Divide chilies among ramekins. Sprinkle with cheese and ham. Blend eggs, cream, salt and pepper in a blender. Divide egg mixture among ramekins, filling ramekins almost to the top. Bake for 35-40 minutes. Serve with guacamole, salsa, sour cream and tomatoes.

Glenelly Inn & Cottages

The Glenelly Inn & Cottages is nestled among ancient oak trees in the enchanting village of Glen Ellen. This Sonoma Wine Country inn is ideal for romantic getaways, honeymoons, winery tours, spa treatments and for those seeking the serenity of the "Valley of the Moon."

Breakfast at the Glenelly Inn is a delicious affair, served in the common room by the cobblestone fireplace or on the flagstone patio, depending on the weather. Tables are set with lovely china, sterling flatware, country-style placemats, cloth napkins and pitchers of fresh juice.

INNKEEPERS:	Kristi Hallamore Jeppesen
ADDRESS:	5131 Warm Springs Road
	Glen Ellen, California 95442
TELEPHONE:	(707) 996-6720
E-MAIL:	glenelly@glenelly.com
WEBSITE:	www.glenelly.com
ROOMS:	6 Rooms; 2 Suites; 2 Cottages; Private baths
CHILDREN:	Welcome
ANIMALS:	Not allowed; Resident dogs & cat
HANDICAPPED:	Handicapped accessible
DIETARY NEEDS:	Will accommodate guests' special dietary needs

Baked Smoked Salmon & Asparagus Eggs Benedict

Makes 6 Servings

3	English muffins, split
5⅓	tablespoons butter, melted
12	asparagus spears (tips plus 2-inches of spears), blanched for 1 minute
¼	pound smoked salmon, cut into pieces
8	eggs
1	cup hollandaise sauce (homemade or from a mix)

Salt & white pepper, to taste
Chopped fresh lemon thyme or tarragon, to taste
Juice of 1 lemon
Lemon slices, for garnish
Sprigs of lemon thyme or tarragon, for garnish

Preheat oven to 400°F. Put English muffins, cut-side-down, in a 9x13-inch baking dish sprayed with non-stick cooking spray. Pour melted butter over English muffins. Top with asparagus and smoked salmon.

In a bowl, combine eggs and hollandaise sauce. Stir in salt, white pepper, lemon thyme or tarragon and lemon juice; pour over ingredients in baking dish. Bake for about 40 minutes, or until egg mixture is set. Cut squares around English muffin halves. Garnish with lemon slices and lemon thyme or tarragon sprigs to serve.

Shaw House Inn

B uilt in 1854 by the city's founder for his bride, the Shaw House Inn, the oldest bed & breakfast in California, served as the first courthouse and post office in Ferndale. This Carpenter Gothic Revival house is a rare find with its jutting gables, balconies and bay windows. A one acre cottage garden surrounds this beautiful home in a timeless, park-like setting.

Fresh fruit and flowers garnish morning culinary treats such as mushroom leek frittata, French bread pudding with homemade berry sauce, cheddar Parmesan strata, crêpes, scones and homemade bread.

INNKEEPERS:	Paula Bigley
ADDRESS:	703 Main Street
	Ferndale, California 95536
TELEPHONE:	(707) 786-9958; (800) 557-7429
E-MAIL:	stay@shawhouse.com
WEBSITE:	www.shawhouse.com
ROOMS:	7 Rooms; 1 Suite; Private baths
CHILDREN:	Welcome
ANIMALS:	Not allowed
HANDICAPPED:	Not handicapped accessible
DIETARY NEEDS:	Will accommodate guests' special dietary needs

Chicken-Apple Sausage Frittata

Makes 5 to 6 Servings

This frittata recipe is from former Shaw House Inn owner Jan Culbert. Serve the frittata with muffins and fresh fruit.

1   large leek (or 1½-2 small leeks), white part only
1   tablespoon olive oil
2   chicken-apple sausages (3-4 ounces each), diced and cooked
¼   cup sour cream
6   large eggs
3-4   leaves fresh basil, minced
Dash of nutmeg
Dash of cayenne pepper
Salt and white pepper, to taste
¾   cup grated Swiss cheese

Preheat oven to 375°F. Slice leek in half lengthwise and wash thoroughly (they are often very sandy.) Dice leek. Heat oil in a skillet over medium heat. Add leek; cook until tender. Remove from heat and stir in sausage.

Whisk together sour cream and eggs. Stir in basil, nutmeg and cayenne. Season with salt and pepper. Stir in cheese. Stir in leek mixture. Pour egg mixture into a greased 9-inch glass pie pan. Bake for about 30 minutes, until set in center.

Old Thyme Inn

Spend enchanted nights in this ideal setting, where time seems to stand still and romance flourishes like fresh hydrangeas. The Old Thyme Inn will wash away your concerns with the everyday and transport you to an elegant world of easy sophistication and charmed relaxation.

The inn's guest rooms take their names from the garden. All are uniquely decorated with lovely antiques, sumptuous beds with crisp cotton linens, original fine art, Essential Elements spa amenities and fresh flowers.

INNKEEPERS:	Kathy & Rick Ellis
ADDRESS:	779 Main Street
	Half Moon Bay, California 94019
TELEPHONE:	(650) 726-1616; (800) 720-4277
E-MAIL:	innkeeper@oldthymeinn.com
WEBSITE:	www.oldthymeinn.com
ROOMS:	7 Rooms; Private baths
CHILDREN:	Welcome
ANIMALS:	Not allowed; Resident dog
HANDICAPPED:	Not handicapped accessible
DIETARY NEEDS:	Will accommodate guests' special dietary needs

Artichoke Frittata

"A healthy and delicious breakfast entrée. Serve with toast and chicken-apple sausage." ~ Innkeeper, Old Thyme Inn

1-2   tablespoons olive oil
4   green onions, finely chopped
2   medium potatoes, diced
1   medium tomato, chopped
1   (14-ounce) can artichoke hearts, quartered
2   tablespoons chopped parsley
Salt and pepper, to taste
¼   cup grated Pecorino Romano cheese
8   large eggs
½   cup half & half
1   cup grated Monterey Jack cheese
Sour cream, for garnish
Fresh herbs (such as basil, lemon thyme or rosemary), for garnish

Preheat oven to 350°F. Spray a 9-inch pie pan with non-stick cooking spray. Heat olive oil in a skillet over medium heat. Add green onions; cook until soft. Add potatoes; cook until golden. Add tomatoes, artichoke hearts and parsley; cook for 2 minutes. Season with salt and pepper. Spread tomato mixture in pie pan. Sprinkle with Romano cheese.

Whisk together eggs and half & half. Season with salt and pepper. Pour egg mixture over ingredients in pie pan. Sprinkle with Monterey Jack cheese. Bake for 30 minutes. Cut quiche into 6 wedges. Garnish with a dab of sour cream and fresh herbs to serve.

Garratt Mansion

The circa 1893 Garratt Mansion is nestled in the quiet community of Alameda, just 12 miles from both San Francisco and Berkeley. This fully restored mansion offers the conveniences of today amid a backdrop of more than 8,000-square-feet of Victorian splendor.

In Diana's Room, the inn's suite, you can write postcards at the large, antique Chinese desk in the sitting room, lounge with a good book in front of the fireplace in the bedroom or soak in the large claw-foot tub. With so many options, you may never want to leave!

INNKEEPERS:	Betty & Royce Gladden
ADDRESS:	900 Union Street
	Alameda, California 94501
TELEPHONE:	(510) 521-4779
E-MAIL:	innkeeper@garrattmansion.com
WEBSITE:	www.garrattmansion.com
ROOMS:	6 Rooms; 1 Suite; Private & shared baths
CHILDREN:	Welcome
ANIMALS:	Not allowed
HANDICAPPED:	Not handicapped accessible
DIETARY NEEDS:	Will accommodate guests' special dietary needs

Basil & Sausage Frittata

Makes 8 to 10 Servings

Basil and sausage sauce:

8	ounces link Italian sausage (Jones sausage is good)
2	tablespoons butter or margarine
1	medium onion, thinly sliced
1	clove garlic, minced
5	medium green, red and/or yellow bell peppers, sliced lengthwise into ¼-inch-thick slices
4	cups medium dice Roma tomatoes
½	cup finely chopped fresh basil
1	tablespoon sugar
1¼	teaspoons salt

Frittata:

1	tablespoon butter or margarine
½	cup finely chopped green onion
10	large eggs
¾	cup sour cream
2	tablespoons finely chopped fresh basil
¾	teaspoon salt
¼	teaspoon black pepper
¾	cup grated Parmesan cheese

For the sauce: Cook sausage in a skillet over medium heat until done; remove from skillet, cool and cut into 1-inch pieces. Melt butter in a skillet over medium heat. Add onion and garlic; cook until onion is translucent. Add bell peppers; cook for 5 minutes. Stir in tomatoes, basil, sugar and salt. Bring to a boil. Add sausage, lower heat and simmer until liquid is reduced by half (sauce can be made ahead, covered and refrigerated, then reheated).

For the frittata: Preheat broiler. Melt butter in a 10-inch, non-stick, oven-proof skillet over medium heat. Add green onion; cook for 1 minute. Whisk together eggs, sour cream, basil, salt and pepper; add to skillet and cook for 8-10 minutes, until eggs are set and light brown on bottom. Remove from heat. Sprinkle with cheese. Place skillet 6-inches from heat in broiler for 2 minutes, until cheese melts. Serve immediately with basil and sausage sauce.

The Seasons

The Seasons Bed & Breakfast is located in the Ollis-Plumado House in the heart of California's Gold Country. This completely remodeled house, one of the city's oldest, was built in 1859. Situated on a beautifully landscaped three-quarter acre lot, just a block from main street, the house is built of brick and placerite stone and was once the site of a gold stamp mill.

"Innkeepers Ken & Bonnie Blosser liken their property to a Tuscan country villa. The Italian theme continues into the morning when frittatas and focaccia are likely to be served for breakfast." ~ *Sacramento Magazine*

INNKEEPERS:	Ken & Bonnie Blosser
ADDRESS:	2934 Bedford Avenue
	Placerville, California 95667
TELEPHONE:	(530) 626-4420
E-MAIL:	theseasons@blosserwest.com
WEBSITE:	www.theseasons.net
ROOMS:	3 Rooms; 1 Suites; 2 Cottages; Private baths
CHILDREN:	Welcome in suite
ANIMALS:	Not allowed
HANDICAPPED:	Not handicapped accessible
DIETARY NEEDS:	Will accommodate guests' special dietary needs

Basil Yogurt Frittata

Makes 3 to 4 Servings

2   tablespoons butter, divided
¼   cup thinly sliced green onions
½   cup plain yogurt
6   eggs, divided
Salt and pepper, to taste
⅓   cup chopped fresh basil
1   tablespoon pine nuts
½   cup freshly grated Parmesan cheese

Preheat oven to 500°F. Melt 1 tablespoon of butter in an oven-proof, 10-inch skillet with sloping sides over medium heat. Add green onions and cook until soft.

In a bowl, beat yogurt with 1 egg. Beat in remaining eggs, 1 at a time, until blended. Add salt, pepper and basil. Add remaining 1 tablespoon of butter to green onions in skillet; heat until melted. Pour egg mixture over green onions. Cook for about 5 minutes, until eggs are softly set, but still moist.

Sprinkle pine nuts over eggs. Remove from heat. Sprinkle Parmesan cheese over all. Transfer skillet to oven and bake until cheese is golden brown.

Dunbar House, 1880

The Dunbar House, 1880 is a historic bed & breakfast inn that offers fine accommodations, gracious hospitality and unforgettable cuisine for travelers headed to California's historic Gold Rush Country. The inn is located in a lush garden setting and offers nearby golf, skiing, restaurants, shopping and world-class wine tasting.

"From the moment you cross the threshold of this country refuge, you will be indulged with old-fashioned hospitality and romance." ~ *Best Places to Stay in California.*

INNKEEPERS:	Barbara & Bob Costa
ADDRESS:	271 Jones Street
	Murphys, California 95247
TELEPHONE:	(209) 728-2897; (800) 692-6006
E-MAIL:	innkeep@dunbarhouse.com
WEBSITE:	www.dunbarhouse.com
ROOMS:	3 Rooms; 2 Suites; Private baths
CHILDREN:	Children age 10 and older welcome
ANIMALS:	Not allowed
HANDICAPPED:	Not handicapped accessible
DIETARY NEEDS:	Will accommodate guests' special dietary needs

Cherry Tomato & Ricotta Omelets in Toast Cups

Makes 6 Servings

"I adapted this recipe from one I found in Cooking *magazine." - Innkeeper, Dunbar House, 1880*

½   stick unsalted butter, divided
6   slices country white bread, cut into 5x3¼-inch rectangles
36   small mixed red and orange cherry tomatoes (about ¾ pound)
12   large eggs
½   cup milk or water
Coarse salt and freshly ground pepper, to taste
⅔   cup ricotta cheese
2   ounces mixed green and red oak leaf lettuce
Olive oil
2   tablespoons chopped chives

Preheat oven to 425°F. Melt 2 tablespoons of butter. Brush melted butter over both sides of each piece of bread. Gently press 1 piece of bread into each of 6 muffin cups, allowing bread to overlap cup slightly. Bake bread until golden, about 10 minutes. Remove from oven and set aside.

Melt remaining 2 tablespoons of butter in a 12-inch skillet over medium heat. Add tomatoes and cook just until soft, about 3 minutes. Whisk together eggs, milk, salt and pepper until light and fluffy, about 2 minutes. Add egg mixture to tomatoes and cook for 3-5 minutes, until eggs begin to set. Lift edge of omelet with a spatula and let uncooked eggs flow underneath. Continue cooking until eggs are almost set. Gently spread ricotta cheese over half of omelet. Fold omelet over and remove from heat.

Put a handful of greens and 1 toast cup on each plate. Divide omelet among toast cups. Drizzle olive oil over greens and omelets. Sprinkle with coarse salt and pepper. Garnish with chopped chives to serve.

The Gables Wine Country Inn

The Gables Wine Country Inn is a beautifully restored, Victorian mansion near Healdsburg, in the center of the Sonoma Wine Country. The inn sits on three and one-half pastoral acres with magnificent vineyard views. A multitude of nearby activities make this inn ideal for everyone from wine and gourmet lovers to those who prefer the outdoors or fine art.

Each spacious bedroom is distinctly appointed with the most tasteful antique and hand-crafted furnishings. Cozy goose-down comforters, fresh cut flowers and a selection of literary classics invite guests to snuggle in.

INNKEEPERS:	Mike & Pam Stanbrough
ADDRESS:	4257 Petaluma Hill Road
	Santa Rosa, California 95404
TELEPHONE:	(707) 585-7777; (800) 422-5376
E-MAIL:	innkeeper@thegablesinn.com
WEBSITE:	www.thegablesinn.com
ROOMS:	4 Rooms; 3 Suites; 1 Cottage; Private baths
CHILDREN:	Welcome
ANIMALS:	Not allowed; Resident cat
HANDICAPPED:	Handicapped accessible
DIETARY NEEDS:	Will accommodate guests' special dietary needs

Sonoma Fumé Scramble

Makes 8 to 10 Servings

White sauce:
2   tablespoons butter
2   tablespoons all-purpose flour
2   cups plus 2 tablespoons milk

Eggs:
½   stick butter
¼   cup chopped green onion
1   pound mushrooms, sliced
18   eggs
¼   cup chopped parsley, plus extra for garnish
½   teaspoon dill weed
⅛   teaspoon pepper
¼   cup Sonoma County Fumé Blanc
1½   cups grated Monterey Jack cheese
1½   cups grated sharp cheddar cheese
Paprika, to taste
Cherry tomatoes or fresh fruit, for garnish

For the white sauce: Melt butter in a saucepan over medium-low heat. Stir in flour until smooth. Cook until bubbly. Whisk in 2 cups of milk until smooth. Lower heat to low and cook, stirring, until thickened; set aside.

For the eggs: Preheat oven to 350°F. Melt butter in a large skillet over medium-low heat. Add green onions and mushrooms; cook until green onions are soft. Beat eggs, 2 tablespoons of milk, parsley, dill and pepper; stir into onion mixture. Cook eggs, gently lifting cooked portion and letting uncooked portion flow underneath, until eggs are just very softly set; remove from heat.

Spoon ½ of eggs into a greased 7x11-inch baking pan. Combine white sauce and wine. Spoon 1 cup of white sauce over eggs. Combine Monterey Jack and cheddar cheese. Sprinkle ½ of cheese mixture over white sauce. Repeat layers. Sprinkle with paprika. Bake for 30-35 minutes, or until hot and bubbly. Let stand for 10 minutes, then cut into squares. Sprinkle with chopped parsley and garnish with cherry tomatoes or fresh fruit.

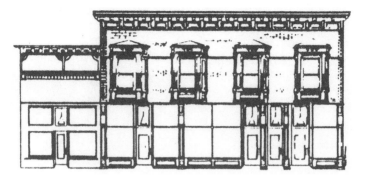

Healdsburg's historic plaza is home to the elegant and charming Healdsburg Inn – "where history and hospitality meet." The many shops, restaurants and wine tasting rooms of Healdsburg are easily explored from the inn. Ascend the grand paneled staircase to the guest suites – most with fireplaces and tubs for two (and with your very own rubber duckie!)

A champagne breakfast is served every morning and a wine tasting is offered every afternoon. A bottomless cookie jar is always available!

INNKEEPERS:	Genny Jenkins
ADDRESS:	110 Matheson Street
	Healdsburg, California 95448
TELEPHONE:	(707) 433-6991; (800) 431-8663
E-MAIL:	innpressions@earthlink.net
WEBSITE:	www.healdsburginn.com
ROOMS:	11 Rooms; Private baths
CHILDREN:	Welcome; Call ahead
ANIMALS:	Not allowed
HANDICAPPED:	Not handicapped accessible
DIETARY NEEDS:	Will accommodate guests' special dietary needs

Fluffy Chile Egg Puff

Makes 6 Servings

5	large eggs
1	cup cottage cheese
1	cup grated Monterey Jack cheese
¼	cup all-purpose flour
2	tablespoons butter, melted
½	teaspoon baking powder
1	(4-ounce) can diced mild green chiles

Preheat oven to 350°F. Spray a 9-inch quiche or pie pan with non-stick cooking spray. Combine all ingredients; pour into pan. Bake for 35 minutes.

Arnold Black Bear Inn

The Black Bear Inn is situated in a park-like setting and is comprised of several new timber-frame buildings that offer a lodge-like feel and an outdoorsy air. Centrally located near restaurants, antique shops, galleries, shopping, golf, skiing and wineries, the town of Arnold's only bed & breakfast is an ideal mountain getaway.

"Thank you for a wonderful time. The rooms are very comfy – especially with all the bear accents. The breakfast was out of this world! We will be back soon." ~ Guests, San Ramon, California

INNKEEPERS:	Doreen & Kirk Swanson
ADDRESS:	1343 Oak Circle
	Arnold, California 95223
TELEPHONE:	(209) 795-8999; (866) 795-8999
E-MAIL:	innkeeper@arnoldblackbearinn.com
WEBSITE:	www.arnoldblackbearinn.com
ROOMS:	5 Rooms; Private baths
CHILDREN:	Not allowed
ANIMALS:	Not allowed; Resident dogs
HANDICAPPED:	Handicapped accessible
DIETARY NEEDS:	Will accommodate guests' special dietary needs

Scrambled Egg Casserole

Makes 6 to 8 Servings

"My mother-in-law would cook this for Christmas brunch. Plan ahead – this dish needs to be refrigerated overnight." – Innkeeper, Arnold Black Bear Inn

Eggs:

3	tablespoons butter or margarine
1	cup chopped ham, Canadian bacon or cooked bacon
¼	cup chopped green onions
½	cup sliced fresh mushrooms
12	eggs

Cheese sauce:

2	tablespoons butter or margarine
2	tablespoons all-purpose flour
2	cups milk
1	cup grated cheddar cheese
¼	teaspoon salt
⅛	teaspoon pepper

Topping:

2¼	cups soft breadcrumbs (from 3 slices of bread)
½	stick butter or margarine, melted
½	teaspoon paprika

For the eggs: Melt butter in a skillet over medium heat. Add ham, green onions and mushrooms; cook until mushrooms are soft. Beat eggs and add to mushroom mixture. Cook until eggs are set; set aside.

For the cheese sauce: Melt butter in a small saucepan over medium-low heat. Whisk in flour and cook until bubbly. Whisk in milk, cheese, salt and pepper until smooth. Lower heat to low and cook, stirring, until thickened. Combine eggs and cheese sauce; pour into a greased 9x13-inch baking pan.

For the topping: Combine all topping ingredients. Sprinkle topping over ingredients in baking pan. Cover and refrigerate overnight. The next day, preheat oven to 350°F. Bake for 30 minutes.

Poppy Hill

Come and enjoy country comfort at the Poppy Hill Bed & Breakfast. This beautifully restored, country home is situated in a quiet garden setting and is elegantly decorated with a stunning collection of American and European antiques and fine art. Guests can explore nearby Yosemite National Park, relax in the spa or just watch the birds.

"What a blessing to return for the second time to such a place of beauty, calm, relaxation and breakfast delights! You are a wonderful hostess – we'll be back!" ~ Guests, Carmel, California

INNKEEPERS:	Mary Ellen Kirn
ADDRESS:	5218 Crystal Aire Drive
	Mariposa, California 95338
TELEPHONE:	(209) 742-6273; (800) 587-6779
E-MAIL:	poppyhill@sierratel.com
WEBSITE:	www.poppyhill.com
ROOMS:	4 Rooms; Private baths
CHILDREN:	Children age 10 and older welcome
ANIMALS:	Not allowed
HANDICAPPED:	Handicapped accessible
DIETARY NEEDS:	Will accommodate guests' special dietary needs

Eggs Picante

Makes 2 to 3 Servings

"This is sooo good and sooo easy!" ~ *Innkeeper, Poppy Hill Bed & Breakfast*

6	large eggs
6	heaping tablespoons plain yogurt
½	cup picante sauce
½	cup grated cheddar and/or Swiss cheese

Preheat oven to 375°F. In a blender, whip eggs and yogurt; pour into a pie pan sprayed with non-stick cooking spray. Bake for 20 minutes, until eggs are set. Spread picante sauce over eggs and sprinkle with cheese. Bake until cheese is melted, about 5 minutes.

Sequoia View Winery

Visitors to Sequoia View Winery enjoy a wonderful 20-acre vineyard, farm and winery near the north entrance of Kings Canyon and Sequoia National Parks. This romantic bed & breakfast offers expansive views of vineyards and mountains by day and stargazing by night.

Each morning, enjoy a full country breakfast with homemade breads and jams, and fresh orange juice from the inn's trees. The winery tasting room offers handcrafted Merlots, Zinfandels and Cabernet Sauvignons, as well as the inn's own rare and unique Rhone-style Alicante Bouschet.

INNKEEPERS:	Jim & Debbie Van Haun
ADDRESS:	1384 Frankwood Avenue
	Sanger, California 93657
TELEPHONE:	(559) 787-9412; (866) 738-6420
E-MAIL:	info@svbnb.com
WEBSITE:	www.svbnb.com
ROOMS:	2 Suites; Private baths
CHILDREN:	Welcome
ANIMALS:	Not allowed; Resident dog
HANDICAPPED:	Not handicapped accessible
DIETARY NEEDS:	Will accommodate guests' special dietary needs

Baked Scrambled Eggs with Canadian Bacon

Makes 4 Servings

"Breakfasts at Sequoia View Winery Bed & Breakfast are always made from scratch. Fresh squeezed orange juice from our own trees, local fruit and this creamy breakfast pie will prepare you for a day of hiking, and then perhaps wine tasting in our new tasting room." - Innkeeper, Sequoia View Winery Bed & Breakfast

4	large eggs, beaten
½	cup Bisquick
½	stick butter, melted
1	cup low-fat cottage cheese
1	cup grated low-fat mozzarella cheese
½	cup skim or 2% milk
6	ounces Canadian bacon, diced

Preheat oven to 350°F. Spray a deep-dish pie pan or an 8x8-inch baking pan with non-stick cooking spray. Combine all ingredients and pour into pan. Bake for 50 minutes. Cool for 10 minutes before slicing and serving.

Cornelius Daly Inn

The Cornelius Daly Inn is an exquisite Colonial Revival circa 1905 mansion built by Cornelius Daly for his wife and their five children. The inn is located in the historic section of Eureka, a few blocks from the Pacific Ocean and a short drive to the majestic redwoods in Humboldt Redwoods State Park and Redwoods National Park.

The inn has been lovingly restored to its original elegance. Original features include four fireplaces and lovely Victorian gardens. Rooms are furnished with turn-of-the-century antiques reflecting the charm of the early 1900s.

INNKEEPERS:	Donna & Bob Gafford
ADDRESS:	1125 H Street
	Eureka, California 95501
TELEPHONE:	(707) 445-3638; (800) 321-9656
E-MAIL:	innkeeper@dalyinn.com
WEBSITE:	www.dalyinn.com
ROOMS:	3 Rooms; 2 Suites; Private baths
CHILDREN:	Children age 12 and older welcome
ANIMALS:	Not allowed
HANDICAPPED:	Not handicapped accessible
DIETARY NEEDS:	Will accommodate guests' special dietary needs

Southwestern Eggs & Chorizo Over Polenta

Makes 8 Servings

3¼	cups water
1	teaspoon salt
1	cup polenta
1	tablespoon butter or olive oil
1	cup sliced mushrooms
1	cup grated cheese (cheddar, pepper Jack or a mixture)
8	chorizo link sausages (removed from casings) or patties (optional)
1	tablespoon vinegar
8	eggs

Salsa, for serving
Sour cream, for serving

Bring water and salt to a boil in a saucepan. Add polenta, lower heat and simmer until polenta is very thick and coming away from sides of pan. Heat butter or oil in a small skillet over medium heat. Add mushrooms and cook until soft. Stir cheese and mushrooms into polenta; cook until cheese is melted and combined.

Lightly spray bottom and sides of an 8x8-inch baking pan with non-stick cooking spray. Spread polenta into an ½-inch-thick layer and set aside until polenta is set (the dish can be prepared to this point the night before, covered and refrigerated).

Preheat broiler. Cook chorizo, if desired, in a skillet over medium heat until done; drain any grease. Bring a saucepan of water and vinegar to a boil. Add eggs and poach until done. Cut polenta into 4 (4x4-inch) squares, then cut each square into 2 triangles. Broil polenta (or cook in a little butter or olive oil) until lightly browned. Put 1 polenta triangle on each plate. Top with chorizo and 1 poached egg. Top egg with salsa and a dollop of sour cream.

Madison Street Inn

The Madison Street Inn is attractively situated on a third of an acre of gardens, about an hour from San Francisco and Monterey. The house has a parlor, sitting area, dining room, pool and spa. Several wineries are scattered nearby and Paramount's Great America and Winchester Mystery House are just minutes away.

Come for the special murder mystery weekend, where guests assume the roles of suspect, sleuth, murderer and even victim, in a mystifying case written by David Landau, creator of the mystery weekend craze.

INNKEEPERS:	Ralph & Theresa Wigginton
ADDRESS:	1390 Madison Street
	Santa Clara, California 95050
TELEPHONE:	(408) 249-5541
E-MAIL:	madstinn@aol.com
WEBSITE:	www.madisonstreetinn.com
ROOMS:	6 Rooms; Private & shared baths
CHILDREN:	Welcome
ANIMALS:	Dogs & cats welcome; Resident dog
HANDICAPPED:	Not handicapped accessible
DIETARY NEEDS:	Will accommodate guests' special dietary needs

Eggs Madison

Makes 4 Servings

4	flour tortillas
2	avocados
2	cups shredded lettuce
1	tablespoon white vinegar
8	eggs
1	cup salsa fresca (fresh salsa) or other salsa
1½	cups grated cheddar cheese
¼	cup sour cream, divided
6	pitted black olives, halved, or more to taste
½	bunch cilantro, chopped or sprigs

Melon or mango slices, for serving

Preheat oven to 200°F. Warm tortillas in oven. Slice avocados in half; pit and peel. Cut each avocado in half horizontally, so you end up with 8 flat slices. Divide lettuce among plates. Put 2 avocado slices on each plate.

Bring a saucepan of water to a simmer. Add vinegar. Add eggs and poach to desired doneness. Warm salsa. Put 1 poached egg in each avocado slice. Top with salsa. Sprinkle with cheese. Top with 1 tablespoon of sour cream and 2 olive halves. Garnish with chopped cilantro or cilantro sprigs. Serve with melon or mango and warmed tortillas folded into fourths.

Note: Tortillas can also be warmed quickly on a griddle or in a dry skillet, about 10 seconds each.

Anderson Creek Inn

The Anderson Creek Inn is located in the Anderson Valley in Northern California. The area is well-known for its many fine wineries, and many guests enjoy touring them. Nearby Hendy Woods State Park is a great place to hike or enjoy a picnic lunch among the redwoods.

Breakfasts feature homemade baked goods and memorable entrées such as croissant French toast with raspberries, blackberries and Mandarin oranges or baked bananas with chantilly cream. After breakfast, stroll around the lovely garden or treat yourself to an in-room massage.

INNKEEPERS:	Jim & Grace Minton
ADDRESS:	12050 Anderson Valley Way
	Boonville, California 95415
TELEPHONE:	(707) 895-3091; (800) 552-6202
E-MAIL:	innkeeper@andersoncreekinn.com
WEBSITE:	www.andersoncreekinn.com
ROOMS:	5 Rooms; Private baths
CHILDREN:	Children age 10 and older welcome
ANIMALS:	Not allowed; Resident dogs & cats
HANDICAPPED:	Not handicapped accessible
DIETARY NEEDS:	Will accommodate guests' special dietary needs

Smoked Salmon & Wild Rice Quiche with Tomato Coulis

Makes 8 Servings

"This is an absolutely delicious quiche on its own, but is spectacular when topped with a tomato coulis." ~ Innkeeper, Anderson Creek Inn

Tomato coulis:

1⅓	cups cherry tomatoes or chopped fresh tomatoes
1	teaspoon balsamic vinegar
½	teaspoon salt
1½	teaspoons olive oil

Purée tomatoes, vinegar, salt and olive oil in a blender until smooth. Strain through a sieve into a bowl, pressing on solids to extract all juices; discard solids. (Coulis will keep refrigerated for several days or it can be frozen.)

Smoked salmon & wild rice quiche:

½	cup wild rice
½	cup brown rice
8	ounces smoked salmon, thinly sliced
1½	cups grated Gruyère cheese
1½	cups grated Jarlsberg cheese
1½	cups half & half
1¼	teaspoons dry mustard
½	teaspoon black pepper
½	teaspoon dill weed
4	large eggs

Preheat oven to 350°F. Cook wild rice and brown rice according to package directions. Cool. Spoon rice over bottom of a buttered 9x13-inch glass baking dish. Top with smoked salmon. Sprinkle with cheeses.

In a saucepan, heat half & half, dry mustard, pepper and dill just to the boiling point; remove from heat. Rapidly beat in egg; pour over ingredients in baking dish. Bake for 35 minutes. Remove from oven and let stand for 10 minutes. Slice and serve topped with tomato coulis.

White Swan Inn

With crackling fireplaces in all 26 guestrooms and suites, the White Swan Inn is a romantic, small hotel in the Nob Hill/Union Square area of San Francisco. The inn is a visually stunning tribute to the intimate hotels of London, with dark wood paneling, rich carpets, comfortable furniture and enchanting English art.

Guests enjoy a lavish, gourmet breakfast buffet and evening wine and hors d'oeuvres served fireside in the cozy parlor.

INNKEEPERS:	Karlene Holloman
ADDRESS:	845 Bush Street
	San Francisco, California 94108
TELEPHONE:	(415) 775-1755; (800) 999-9570
E-MAIL:	kh@jdvhospitality.com
WEBSITE:	www.whiteswaninnsf.com
ROOMS:	26 Rooms; Private baths
CHILDREN:	Children welcome
ANIMALS:	Not allowed
HANDICAPPED:	Not handicapped accessible
DIETARY NEEDS:	Will accommodate guests' special dietary needs

Mushroom Quiche

Makes 6 to 8 Servings

"This has been our most popular breakfast item for over 20 years." ~ Innkeeper, White Swan Inn

1	tablespoon butter
½	pound mushrooms, sliced
½	medium onion, chopped
1	cup grated Swiss cheese
½	cup grated Parmesan cheese
½	teaspoon thyme
½	teaspoon oregano
8	large eggs
2	cups milk
1	cup heavy cream

Salt and pepper, to taste

Preheat oven to 375°F. Melt butter in a skillet over medium heat. Add mushrooms and onions; cook until soft. Spread ½ of Swiss cheese and ½ of Parmesan cheese in bottom of a greased quiche or pie pan. Top with mushroom mixture. Sprinkle with remaining Swiss and Parmesan cheese. Sprinkle with thyme and oregano.

Whisk together eggs, milk, cream, salt and pepper; pour over ingredients in pan. Bake for 35-45 minutes, until set and golden brown.

1801 First

This luxurious Napa Valley bed & breakfast inn welcomes guests to a world of casual elegance and relaxed refinement in Wine Country. 1801 First caters to your every luxurious whim. Each bath pampers you with an oversized soaking tub and spacious, separate shower or Jacuzzi. Sensual bath amenities and soothing robes complete the experience.

In each room, exquisite beds are lavishly adorned with fine linens, down comforters and Egyptian cotton coverlets. Romantic fireplaces and inviting sitting areas encourage lazy, tranquil afternoons.

INNKEEPERS:	Darcy & Tom Tunt
ADDRESS:	1801 First Street
	Napa, California 94559
TELEPHONE:	(707) 224-3939; (800) 518-0146
E-MAIL:	info@1801first.com
WEBSITE:	www.1801first.com
ROOMS:	5 Suites; 2 Cottages; 1 Guest House; Private baths
CHILDREN:	Children not allowed
ANIMALS:	Not allowed
HANDICAPPED:	Handicapped accessible
DIETARY NEEDS:	Will accommodate guests' special dietary needs

Caramelized Onion, Spinach & Blue Cheese Quiche

Makes 8 Servings

2	tablespoons olive oil
4	white onions, thinly sliced
1	teaspoon sugar
⅓	cup dry red wine
3	tablespoons unsalted butter
1	(10-ounce) package frozen spinach, thawed and squeezed dry

Salt and pepper, to taste
Pinch of nutmeg

6	ounces strong blue cheese, such as Roquefort or Stilton
¾	cup heavy cream
4	large eggs, beaten
1	unbaked pie crust

Orange slices, for garnish
Rosemary sprigs, for garnish

Preheat oven to 350°F. Heat oil in a skillet over medium-low heat. Add onions and cook gently for 8 minutes, or until translucent. Raise heat to medium, add sugar and cook for 5-10 minutes longer, until onions are golden brown and sweet. Add wine and cook until onions are soft and liquid has evaporated. Season with salt and pepper. Remove from skillet and set aside.

In skillet used to cook onions, melt butter over medium-high heat. Add spinach and cook, stirring constantly, until spinach is dry when pressed with the back of a spoon. Season with salt, pepper and nutmeg.

Combine blue cheese and cream in a small saucepan over low heat. Cook, stirring, until cheese is melted and combined (do not boil). Cool, then add eggs and mix well. Put onions, then spinach in crust; smooth surface, but do not pack down. Pour cream mixture over ingredients in crust. Bake for 45-60 minutes, until center is set.

Chichester-McKee House

Step into the charm and beauty of another era at the Chichester-McKee House, a historic inn on California's Gold Coast. This lovingly restored, grand Victorian home offers fragrant gardens, Victorian antiques and the splendor of the Sierra Nevada foothills.

Spend the day exploring historic Placerville, or head off for an adventure of rafting or gold panning. Return to the inn and enjoy bedrooms with period furniture and soft robes hanging in an elegant armoire – truly the lap of Victorian luxury!

INNKEEPERS:	Doreen & Bill Thornhill
ADDRESS:	800 Spring Street
	Placerville, California 95667
TELEPHONE:	(530) 626-1882; (800) 831-4008
E-MAIL:	info@innlover.com
WEBSITE:	www.innlover.com
ROOMS:	4 Rooms; Private baths
CHILDREN:	Children welcome
ANIMALS:	Not allowed; Resident dog
HANDICAPPED:	Not handicapped accessible
DIETARY NEEDS:	Will accommodate guests' special dietary needs

Ham & Asparagus Crêpes

Makes 6 Servings

Crêpes:
1   cup milk
3   large eggs
⅔   cup all-purpose flour

Filling:
12   thin slices Black Forest ham
4   slices Muenster cheese, cut into thirds
24-36 asparagus spears, steamed, or 3 (15-ounce) cans asparagus spears
Paprika, for garnish

Cheese sauce:
3   tablespoons butter, melted
3   tablespoons all-purpose flour
1   cup milk
1   cup grated sharp cheddar cheese
Dash of white pepper

For the crêpes: Blend all crêpe ingredients in a blender; let stand for 30 minutes. Heat a lightly greased, 8-inch crêpe pan or skillet over medium-high heat. Pour a little batter into pan. Rotate pan so batter covers bottom of pan. Cook until bubbles appear and edges start to brown. Turn and cook other side for a few seconds. Stack cooked crêpes between waxed paper.

For the filling: Preheat oven to 325°F. Put a slice of ham, ⅓ slice of cheese and 2-3 asparagus spears on each crêpe. Roll up crêpes and place in a 9x13-inch baking pan. Cover with foil. (Crêpes may be prepared ahead to this point, covered and refrigerated overnight.) Bake for 25 minutes. Uncover pan and bake for 5 minutes longer. Serve 2 crêpes per person, topped with 2-3 tablespoons of cheese sauce and a sprinkle of paprika.

For the cheese sauce: Combine butter, flour and milk; whisk until smooth. Microwave for 3 minutes. Stir in cheese and white pepper. Microwave for 2 minutes, then whisk again. Microwave for 1 minute at a time until mixture is the consistency of a thin or thick pudding, to your taste.

Villa De Valor

Treat your senses to a step back in time, to memories of the turn of the century. Villa De Valor Bed & Breakfast, located in the heart of Julian, is a formal, Victorian home full of charm and elegance, known in its heyday as the most elegant home in Julian. The inn's gracious front porch is perfect for relaxing and enjoying the beautiful mountain top views. An inviting hammock awaits you on the side of the house.

Located an hour from San Diego at 4,200 feet, guests can enjoy gold mine and winery tours, shopping, carriage rides and mountain trails.

INNKEEPERS:	Valorie Ashley
ADDRESS:	2020 Third Street
	Julian, California 92036
TELEPHONE:	(760) 765-3865; (877)-968-4552
E-MAIL:	villadevalor@aol.com
WEBSITE:	www.villadevalor.com
ROOMS:	3 Suites; Private baths
CHILDREN:	Children age 13 and older welcome
ANIMALS:	Not allowed
HANDICAPPED:	Not handicapped accessible
DIETARY NEEDS:	Will accommodate guests' special dietary needs

Cheese Blintz Egg Soufflé

Makes 6 Servings

"My mom felt that food was too precious to practice on. Therefore, we were not allowed to cook, just watch – and I did. I watched my mom and my grandmothers cook during many hours in the kitchen. They were all great cooks and cooked by 'a bit of this' and a 'little of that' – no recipes. Hence, it is the way I cook today. I serve this soufflé with potatoes, a meat, homemade biscuits and fried peaches." – Innkeeper, Villa de Valor Bed & Breakfast

4	extra-large eggs
⅓	cup half & half
1	tablespoon sour cream

Salt and pepper, to taste
Lawry's seasoning salt, to taste

6	frozen cheese blintzes
1½	tablespoons unsalted butter

Grated Monterey Jack and mild cheddar cheese

Preheat oven to 400°F. Beat eggs well with a whisk. Add half & half and sour cream; beat well. Add several shakes of salt, pepper and seasoning salt; beat again – you should feel it in your wrist.

Spray a soufflé dish with non-stick cooking spray. Put blintzes in dish in a "wagon wheel" pattern. Place butter pieces between blintzes. Put a handfull of each cheese between each blintz (this will keep them in place). Pour egg mixture over and between blintzes. Bake for about 40 minutes, until soufflé rises and top glows with a golden yellow, orange-ish tan. Cut soufflé into 6 wedges and serve.

The Inn at Occidental

Each room and suite at the Inn at Occidental is distinctly different. Select the one that sparks your imagination and discover a treasure trove of whimsical folk art, family heirlooms and rare antique-shop finds. All rooms feature overstuffed down beds, comfortable sitting areas and fireplaces. Most rooms offer spa tubs for two, and many have private decks.

Beautifully prepared and presented, each day's fare is a feast for the eyes and the palate. Executive chef Jan Messersmith creates marvelous dishes with herbs from the inn's gardens and produce from the best Sonoma farms.

INNKEEPERS:	Jerry & Tina Wolsborn
ADDRESS:	3657 Church Street
	Occidental, California 95465
TELEPHONE:	(707) 874-1047; (800) 522-6324
E-MAIL:	innkeeper@innatoccidental.com
WEBSITE:	www.innatoccidental.com
ROOMS:	15 Rooms; 3 Suites; 1 Cottage; Private baths
CHILDREN:	Children age 12 and older welcome
ANIMALS:	Small dogs in cottage only; Resident dogs
HANDICAPPED:	Handicapped accessible
DIETARY NEEDS:	Will accommodate guests' special dietary needs

Chilaquiles

Makes 4 Servings

"While trying to think of a new breakfast item that would reflect our Sonoma County area, the Tex-Mex breakfast dish, "Migas" came to mind and our chef, Jan, came up with this recipe." ~ Innkeeper, The Inn at Occidental

3	tablespoons vegetable oil
3	corn tortillas, sliced into 1-inch-thick strips
1	medium onion, chopped
8	eggs, beaten
1	medium tomato, chopped into ¼-inch dice
½	cup chopped cilantro
1	cup grated Monterey Jack cheese

Salt and pepper, to taste

1	cup fresh salsa, for serving
½	cup sour cream, for serving

Heat oil in a large skillet over medium heat. Add tortilla strips and onion; cook until onion is slightly browned. Whisk eggs. Add tomatoes and pour mixture into skillet. Using a spatula, push cooked eggs toward center, turning eggs in large spoonfuls (do not scramble eggs or break up tortillas).

When eggs are almost done, stir in cilantro and cheese. Season with salt and pepper. Lower heat to low. Cover skillet and cook for 1-2 minutes, until cheese is melted. Cut into 4 wedges. Serve with salsa and sour cream.

Note: Ingredients can be divided into 4 parts and cooked in a small skillet to make individual servings.

The Bissell House

During the late 19th century, Pasadena's Orange Grove Avenue was lined with beautiful mansions, some of which still stand. Built in 1887, the Bissell House Bed & Breakfast has been the southern anchor of this famous street, which was traditionally referred to as "Millionaire's Row."

"A beautiful home filled with care and attention. It was a pleasure to stay where we were made to feel welcome and pampered. Our room was large, beautifully decorated, with a large closet and lovely, old-fashioned bath. We couldn't have been happier." ~Guests, Evanston, Illinois

INNKEEPERS:	Russell & Leonore Butcher
ADDRESS:	201 Orange Grove Avenue
	South Pasadena, California 91030
TELEPHONE:	(626) 441-3535; (800) 441-3530
E-MAIL:	info@bissellhouse.com
WEBSITE:	www.bissellhouse.com
ROOMS:	5 Rooms; 1 Suite; Private baths
CHILDREN:	Children age 10 and older welcome
ANIMALS:	Not allowed
HANDICAPPED:	Not handicapped accessible
DIETARY NEEDS:	Will accommodate guests' special dietary needs

Torta Piazzano

Makes 8 Servings

6	large russet (baking) potatoes
¾	stick butter, divided, plus 2 tablespoons butter, chilled
1	medium onion, chopped
6	eggs
⅓	cup half & half
1	teaspoon Santa Maria seasoning
¼	cup crumbled blue cheese
3	huge handfuls fresh spinach, washed and stemmed

Phyllo dough

¼	cup grated Parmesan cheese

Preheat oven to 400°F. Microwave potatoes for 12-15 minutes, until almost soft. Melt 4 tablespoons of butter in a skillet over medium heat. Add onions; cook until translucent. Dice potatoes and add to skillet; cook until done, then cool slightly. Beat eggs, half & half and Santa Maria seasoning. Stir in blue cheese and spinach; add to warm (not hot) potato mixture and stir to combine.

Butter bottom and sides of a springform pan. Melt remaining 2 tablespoons of butter. Put 1 sheet of phyllo dough in pan. Brush with melted butter. Repeat until you have a stack of 4 sheets and bottom of pan is completely covered. Press potato mixture solidly into pan over phyllo. Sprinkle with Parmesan cheese. Scrape 2 tablespoons of chilled butter onto inside of pan to crisp edges of dish. Bake for 10 minutes. Lower oven temperature to 350°F and bake for 30 minutes longer, until top is golden brown.

*Note: Santa Maria Seasoning is a garlic salt and pepper blend. It is available in larger groceries, many Costcos or at www.susieqbrand.com.

Green Gables Inn

With its spectacular setting at water's edge, the Green Gables Inn is one of the most beautiful and famous inns in California. Every detail in this exquisite, circa 1888, Queen Anne Victorian has been meticulously restored. Visiting this historic gem, with its panoramic views of Monterey Bay, is an experience guests never forget.

In the morning, breakfast is served in the dining room overlooking the rocky coastline. Each afternoon, wine and hors d'oeuvres are are set out in front of a fire in the parlor.

INNKEEPERS:	Lucia Root
ADDRESS:	301 Ocean Avenue
	Pacific Grove, California 93950
TELEPHONE:	(831) 375-2095; (800) 722-1774
E-MAIL:	greengablesinn@foursisters.com
WEBSITE:	www.foursisters.com
ROOMS:	11 Rooms; Private & shared baths
CHILDREN:	Children welcome
ANIMALS:	Not allowed
HANDICAPPED:	Not handicapped accessible
DIETARY NEEDS:	Will accommodate guests' special dietary needs

Hobo Breakfast

Makes 4 to 8 Servings

2	tablespoons butter, divided
1	large onion, chopped
1	tablespoon vegetable oil
5	large red potatoes, cooked until tender and diced
1	teaspoon paprika

Salt and pepper, to taste

3	tablespoons chopped parsley
8	eggs
1	tablespoon white vinegar
1	cup grated cheddar cheese

Cream sauce:

½	stick butter
½	cup all-purpose flour
1	cup half & half, or more if needed
1	tablespoon lemon juice
¼	cup crumbled cooked bacon (optional)

Salt and pepper, to taste

Melt 1 tablespoon of butter in a skillet over medium heat. Add onions and cook until soft; remove and set aside. Melt remaining 1 tablespoon of butter with oil in a large skillet over medium heat; add potatoes, paprika, salt and pepper. Cook, stirring as little as possible, until potatoes are browned and crisp. Stir in parsley and onions.

Preheat oven to 350°F. Layer potatoes in a quiche or pie pan and reheat in oven. Top with cheese and bake until cheese is melted. Fill a saucepan half-full with water. Add vinegar and bring to a boil. Crack eggs gently into water. Poach eggs for about 3 minutes; remove carefully with a slotted spoon. Divide potatoes between plates. Gently place poached eggs on top of potatoes. Top with cream sauce.

For the cream sauce: Melt butter in a saucepan over medium heat. Add flour and cook, stirring constantly, for 2-3 minutes. Add half & half; cook until thickened (add more half & half, if needed). Add lemon juice and bacon bits. Season with salt and pepper. Add cheese; cook until melted and combined.

Johnson's Country Inn

Johnson's Country Inn is located in Chico, in the Sacramento Valley of Northern California. Country quiet surrounds this Victorian farmhouse, which lies within peaceful almond orchards. The history and natural beauty of the valley makes this a marvelous destination. Nearby Bidwell Park offers 3,700 acres for picnicking, swimming, golf and hiking.

Chico's pedestrian-friendly and vibrant downtown area offers shopping, fine and casual dining and theatre, art and music performances.

INNKEEPERS:	Joan & David Johnson
ADDRESS:	3935 Morehead Avenue
	Chico, California 95928
TELEPHONE:	(530) 345-7829
E-MAIL:	j.c.inn@pobox.com
WEBSITE:	www.chico.com/johnsonsinn
ROOMS:	4 Rooms; Private baths
CHILDREN:	Children age 10 and older welcome
ANIMALS:	Not allowed; Resident dog & cat
HANDICAPPED:	Handicapped accessible
DIETARY NEEDS:	Will accommodate guests' special dietary needs

Chile Relleno Casserole

Makes 8 Servings

"Inn guests are especially fond of this recipe. In fact, I have given it to many, many guests over the years. It is not too spicy, even for the most sensitive palates. I serve it with a mango salsa." - Innkeeper, Johnson's Country Inn

1	(18-ounce) can chopped mild green chiles
8	corn tortillas, cut into wide strips
1½	pounds pepper Jack cheese, grated
2	tomatoes, sliced, plus extra tomato slices or wedges, for garnish
12	large eggs
1	clove garlic, minced
¾	cup milk
½	teaspoon salt
½	teaspoon pepper
1	teaspoon cumin

Cilantro sprigs, for garnish
Mango or tomato salsa, for serving

Preheat oven to 350°F. Grease a 9x13-inch baking pan. Spread ½ of chiles in bottom of pan. Top with ½ of tortilla strips and ½ of cheese. Cover with tomato slices. Repeat layers with remaining chiles, tortilla strips and cheese.

Beat together eggs, garlic, milk, salt, pepper and cumin; pour over ingredients in pan. Bake for 1 hour, or until puffy and hot. Let stand for 5-10 minutes before slicing. Garnish with cilantro sprigs and serve with tomato slices or wedges and mango or tomato salsa.

Hanford House Inn

The Hanford House is a classic, ivy-covered, red brick inn filled with light, laughter, great food and personal attention. The inn's spacious rooms blend the elegance of a gracious past with present day comforts. Amenities include a roof-top sun deck overlooking the hills and a shaded patio on which to enjoy a good book.

After a full, gourmet breakfast, you can pan for gold, visit a few of the many local wineries, browse through antique and specialty shops or tour historic Gold Rush buildings and sites.

INNKEEPERS:	Bob & Karen Tierno
ADDRESS:	61 Hanford Street
	Sutter Creek, California 95685
TELEPHONE:	(209) 267-0747; (800) 871-5839
E-MAIL:	info@hanfordhouse.com
WEBSITE:	www.hanfordhouse.com
ROOMS:	7 Rooms; 3 Suites; Private baths
CHILDREN:	Welcome
ANIMALS:	Not allowed; Resident cat
HANDICAPPED:	Handicapped accessible
DIETARY NEEDS:	Will accommodate guests' special dietary needs

Tahoe Brunch Casserole

Makes 8 Servings

Plan ahead – this dish needs to be started the night before.

2-3 tablespoons butter or margarine, softened, plus 1 stick butter
12 slices white bread, crusts removed
½ pound mushrooms, trimmed and sliced
2 cups thinly sliced yellow onion
Salt and pepper, to taste
1½ pounds bulk mild Italian sausage, browned
¾-1 pound cheddar cheese, grated*
5 eggs
2½ cups milk
1 tablespoon Dijon mustard
1 teaspoon dry mustard
1 teaspoon nutmeg
1 teaspoon salt
⅛ teaspoon pepper
2 tablespoons finely chopped parsley

Butter bread with 2-3 tablespoons of butter; set aside. Melt 1 stick of butter in a large skillet over medium heat. Add mushrooms and onions; cook for 5-8 minutes, until tender. Season with salt and pepper. In a 9x13-inch baking dish, layer ½ of bread, ½ of mushroom mixture, ½ of sausage and ½ of cheese. Repeat layers.

Combine eggs, milk, Dijon and dry mustard, nutmeg, salt and pepper. Pour egg mixture over ingredients in baking dish. Cover and refrigerate overnight.

The next day, preheat oven to 350°F. Uncover baking dish and sprinkle with parsley. Bake for 1 hour, or until bubbly. Serve immediately with fruit salad and crusty rolls.

*Tip: For a smoother texture, substitute ½ cheddar cheese and ½ Velveeta, plus ¼ cup vermouth (optional) for the cheddar cheese.

The Shore House at Lake Tahoe

The Shore House at Lake Tahoe, located on the north shore of beautiful Lake Tahoe, is the ultimate Northern California vacation getaway, centrally located near all the lake and mountain activities. Surrounding each floor, balconies and decks offer fabulous panoramic views of the pristine lake and surrounding snow-capped Sierra Nevada mountains.

Each guest room is decorated with knotty pine walls, custom-built log furniture and Scandia Down comforters and featherbeds. A large, outdoor hot tub by the lake is the perfect place to enjoy a gorgeous Tahoe sunset.

INNKEEPERS:	Barb & Marty Cohen
ADDRESS:	7170 North Lake Boulevard
	Tahoe Vista, California 96148
TELEPHONE:	(530) 546-7270; (800) 207-5160
E-MAIL:	barb@shorehouselaketahoe.com
WEBSITE:	www.shorehouselaketahoe.com
ROOMS:	8 Rooms; 1 Cottage; Private baths
CHILDREN:	Welcome
ANIMALS:	Not allowed; Resident dog
HANDICAPPED:	Handicapped accessible
DIETARY NEEDS:	Will accommodate guests' special dietary needs

Sweet Hot Monte Cristo

Makes 1 Serving

"Ah, the sweet taste of success! This recipe won first prize in the 1998 American Bed & Breakfast Recipe Cookoff. When they announced my name, I nearly fell off my chair, and I was sure Bert Parks was going to come out, walk me down the aisle and sing, 'Here she is, Miss America.' I got my taste of fame when I got to bake this on TV. I owe it all to my dad, who died in 1993. He made his own mustards, and because of him, I love using mustards in my recipes – thanks, Dad." ~ Innkeeper, Shore House at Lake Tahoe

1	teaspoon sweet-hot mustard
2	slices sourdough bread
2	slices Muenster cheese
2	slices Canadian bacon
3	thin slices tart green apple
2	eggs, lightly beaten
2	tablespoons low-fat milk
2	tablespoons real maple syrup
1	fresh strawberry, sliced

Powdered sugar, for garnish

Preheat oven to 400°F. Spread mustard over 1 slice of bread. Top with cheese, Canadian bacon, apple and the second slice of bread.

In a shallow baking pan or dish, combine eggs and milk. Soak sandwich in egg mixture for 2 minutes. Turn and soak other side for 2 minutes. Put sandwich on a baking sheet sprayed with non-stick cooking spray.

Bake on each side for about 10 minutes, or until sandwich is browned and cheese is melted. Cut sandwich into triangles. Drizzle with maple syrup, garnish with sliced strawberries and sprinkle with powdered sugar.

The Gate House Inn

The Gate House Inn is a historic mansion set among landscaped lawns and gardens and surrounded by quiet and serene countryside. Go back in time as you read by imported Italian marble fireplaces or sit on expansive porches and watch for deer and wild turkeys. Sun by the large pool or simply relax and immerse yourself in the elegance of days gone by.

A full breakfast features homemade breads or muffins, chicken or turkey sausage, fresh fruit and parfaits, quiches, breakfast casseroles and, of course, the Gate House Inn specialty – baked French toast.

INNKEEPERS:	Mark & Donna Macola
ADDRESS:	1330 Jackson Gate Road
	Jackson, California 95642
TELEPHONE:	(209) 223-3500; (800) 841-1072
E-MAIL:	info@gatehouseinn.com
WEBSITE:	www.gatehouseinn.com
ROOMS:	3 Rooms; 1 Suite; 2 Cottages; Private baths
CHILDREN:	Children age 13 and older welcome; Call ahead
ANIMALS:	Not allowed
HANDICAPPED:	Not handicapped accessible
DIETARY NEEDS:	Will accommodate guests' special dietary needs

Asparagus & Sausage Strata

Makes 8 Servings

Plan ahead – this dish needs to be started the night before.

7	slices Texas toast bread (crusts removed), buttered on 1 side
1	pound bulk breakfast sausage, cooked, crumbled and drained
1½	cups grated cheddar cheese
6	eggs
2	cups milk or half & half
1	teaspoon salt
1	(4-ounce) can chopped mild green chilies
1	(2-ounce) jar sliced pimentos, drained
1	(3-ounce) can chopped ripe black olives
9	ounces fresh asparagus or 1 (14-ounce) can asparagus, drained

Fit bread, buttered-side-up, in a single layer in a 9x13-inch baking dish. Spread sausage over bread. Sprinkle cheese over sausage. Combine eggs, milk, salt, green chilies, pimentos and olives; pour over ingredients in baking dish. Top with asparagus spears. Cover and refrigerate overnight. The next day, preheat oven to 350°F. Bake for 45 minutes.

Inn at Playa Del Rey

Overlooking the sailboats of a main channel of Marina del Rey and set on 300 acres of natural marshes is a place where life seems simpler. Recently named by Forbes.com as "One of the Nation's Top Ten Urban Inns," the Inn at Playa del Rey is a New England-style beach house ideally located just three blocks from the ocean and 15 minutes from Manhattan Beach, Venice Beach and Santa Monica.

The inn's romantic suites are rich in sumptuous detail and feature Jacuzzi tubs, fireplaces, marina views, balconies, king-size canopy feather beds.

INNKEEPERS:	Heather Suskin
ADDRESS:	435 Culver Boulevard
	Playa Del Rey, California 90293
TELEPHONE:	(310) 574-1920
E-MAIL:	info@innatplayadelrey.com
WEBSITE:	www.innatplayadelrey.com
ROOMS:	19 Rooms; 2 Suites; Private baths
CHILDREN:	Welcome
ANIMALS:	Not allowed
HANDICAPPED:	Handicapped accessible
DIETARY NEEDS:	Will accommodate guests' special dietary needs

Sausage Chile Rellenos with Apricots & Raisins

Makes 10 to 12 Servings

1   tablespoon butter, plus extra for buttering baking dish
½   cup chopped onion
1   pound bulk sausage
¼   cup finely chopped (into raisin-size pieces) dried apricots
¼   cup raisins
¼   cup pine nuts, toasted
1   (19-ounce) can mild whole green chiles
1   cup grated Monterey Jack cheese
8   eggs
2   cups milk
Salt and pepper, to taste
1   cup all-purpose flour
Tomatillo salsa or chile con queso (Mexican cheese sauce), for serving

Melt butter in a skillet over medium heat. Add onion and cook until translucent. Add sausage; cook until done, then crumble. Remove from heat and drain grease. Stir in apricots, raisins and pine nuts.

Preheat oven to 375°F. Butter bottom of a 9x13-inch baking dish. Spread chiles over bottom of baking dish. Top with sausage mixture and sprinkle with cheese.

Beat eggs, milk, salt and pepper. Slowly add flour, beating well. Pour egg mixture over ingredients in baking dish; spread to create an even layer. Bake for 45 minutes, until eggs are set. Slice and serve with tomatillo salsa or chile con queso.

Side Dishes & Sauces

Side Dishes
&
Sauces

DeHaven Valley Farm

Meals at DeHaven Valley Farm are freshly made, and many ingredients come from the inn's garden. The innkeepers are committed to preparing exceptional cuisine and supporting sustainable agriculture and organic farming. Chef Rebecca Warda has worked with some of the nation's top chefs at the Pebble Beach Pro-Am and the St. Regis in Laguna Niguel.

Take the inn's private trail along the crystal-clear DeHaven Creek that runs year-round through the middle of the property. You can see the creek's final exit into the Pacific Ocean as it flows underneath Highway 1.

INNKEEPERS:	R. Michael McDonald & Bill Lee-Sammons
ADDRESS:	39247 North Highway One
	Westport, California 95488
TELEPHONE:	(707) 961-1660; (877) 334-2836
E-MAIL:	info@dehavenvalleyfarm.com
WEBSITE:	www.dehavenvalleyfarm.com
ROOMS:	6 Rooms; 3 Cottages; Private & shared baths
CHILDREN:	Welcome
ANIMALS:	Welcome in cottages; Call ahead
HANDICAPPED:	Not handicapped accessible
DIETARY NEEDS:	Will accommodate guests' special dietary needs

Potato Cake with Bacon & Blue Cheese

Makes 4 to 6 Servings

This potato cake is delicious served with Roast Beef Tenderloin with Mushroom Cabernet Sauce (see recipe on page 233).

3   pounds russet potatoes, peeled and cut into 1-inch cubes
2   tablespoons vegetable oil
¼   pound bacon, chopped into ¼-inch dice
½   stick butter, melted plus ½ stick butter, cut into pieces
¼   cup minced shallots
1   tablespoon minced garlic
¼   pound blue cheese, crumbled
Salt and pepper, to taste

Preheat oven to 350°F. Bring a large pot of lightly salted water to a boil. Add potatoes and cook for 5-8 minutes, until about half-done. Remove from heat and drain well.

Cook bacon in a skillet over medium-high heat until lightly browned. Remove and drain on paper towels. Combine bacon, potatoes, melted butter, blue cheese, shallots, garlic and chives; stir gently to combine. Season with salt and pepper.

Spread bacon mixture in an oven-proof skillet, pressing down to compress mixture. Dot cut up butter around edge of skillet. Transfer skillet to oven and bake for about 20 minutes, until golden brown. Remove skillet from oven and let potato cake stand for 5 minutes before slicing and serving.

Orchard Hill Country Inn

The award-winning Orchard Hill Country Inn is located in the heart of Julian's Historic District. The inn offers accommodations of casual elegance where you can relax, unwind and savor an atmosphere designed with your comfort in mind. The inn welcomes guests with exacting service, attention to detail and the hospitality you expect from a fine country inn.

"Sit under the star-studded sky gazing at Julian's few lights peeping through the trees. Toast the prospectors who mined this fine mountain gem and the Straubes for polishing it." ~ *Country Inn's Magazine*

INNKEEPERS:	The Straube Family
ADDRESS:	2502 Washington Street
	Julian, California 92036
TELEPHONE:	(760) 765-1700
E-MAIL:	information@orchardhill.com
WEBSITE:	www.orchardhill.com
ROOMS:	22 Rooms; Private baths
CHILDREN:	Welcome
ANIMALS:	Not allowed
HANDICAPPED:	Handicapped accessible
DIETARY NEEDS:	Will accommodate guests' special dietary needs

Hash Brown Casserole

Makes 8 Servings

3	tablespoons olive oil, divided
1	onion, chopped
1	(16-ounce) package frozen hash browns, thawed
12	eggs
1	cup sour cream
16	slices bacon, cooked crisp and crumbled
3	cups grated cheddar cheese
1	bunch green onions, sliced

Preheat oven to 375°F. Heat 2 tablespoons of oil in a small skillet over medium heat. Add onions and cook until soft. Spray a 7x11-inch baking dish with non-stick cooking spray. Toss hash browns with remaining 1 tablespoon of oil. Combine onions and hash browns; spread in baking dish. Bake for 30-40 minutes, until hash browns are browned.

Scramble eggs and sprinkle or spread over hash brown mixture in baking dish. Spread a thin layer of sour cream over eggs (reserve some sour cream for garnish). Sprinkle bacon, then cheese over sour cream (the dish can be prepared to this point, covered and refrigerated overnight). Bake for 30 minutes (do not overcook). Top each serving with a dollop of sour cream and some green onions.

Bartels' Vineyard Ranch

Located in the heart of Napa Valley, Bartels' Vineyard Ranch and Bed & Breakfast Country Inn is tucked away from the bustle of town, yet is just six minutes from St. Helena's finest restaurants, wineries and shops. The inn's 60-acre country estate overlooks a 100-acre valley surrounded by private vineyards and breathtaking views. Guests can watch horses and deer graze in peaceful meadows from this romantic, hillside hideaway.

Bartels' inviting accommodations feature a collection of original art, floral wall coverings, Persian rug accents and warm Wine Country colors.

INNKEEPERS:	Jami Bartels
ADDRESS:	1200 Conn Valley Road
	St. Helena, California 94574
TELEPHONE:	(707) 963 4001
E-MAIL:	jami@bartelsranch.com
WEBSITE:	www.bartelsranch.com
ROOMS:	4 Rooms; 1 Suites; Private baths
CHILDREN:	Welcome
ANIMALS:	Not allowed; Resident cats, horse, bird sanctuary
HANDICAPPED:	Handicapped accessible
DIETARY NEEDS:	Will accommodate guests' special dietary needs

Jami's Potatoes Magnifique

Makes 8 to 10 Servings

"These amazing potatoes are great for parties, breakfast or dinner. Quick and easy to prepare, and very rich!" ~ Innkeeper, Bartels Vineyard Ranch & Bed & Breakfast Country Inn

5	baking potatoes, boiled and sliced (peeled or unpeeled)
1	cup sour cream
½	(8-ounce) package cream cheese
¼	cup chopped pimentos
½	large red or Vidalia onion, thinly sliced

Curry powder, to taste
Salt and cayenne pepper, to taste
Chopped fresh or dried thyme, to taste
Chopped parsley, to taste
Sliced or chopped fresh basil, to taste

¾	pound sharp cheddar cheese, grated

Paprika, for garnish

Preheat oven to 350°F. In a buttered 5-quart casserole dish, layer ingredients in the following order: potatoes, sour cream, cream cheese, pimentos and onion. Lightly sprinkle with curry powder, salt, cayenne, thyme, parsley and basil. Repeat layers and seasoning until potatoes are used up. Sprinkle with cheese. Sprinkle paprika over entire casserole. Bake for 20 minutes, or until casserole is bubbly and cheese has melted.

Sand Rock Farm

Historic Sand Rock Farm is the perfect Santa Cruz bed & breakfast because of its ideal location just outside the city. A fusion of country inn and European retreat, the inn provides an unparalled blend of gracious hospitality and a serene environment.

Start a relaxed day with an early morning stroll through the fields, or read the paper on the deck overlooking the beautiful gardens. A gourmet array of seasonal treats awaits, such as a warm, cinnamon-laced morning bun followed by a delicious entrée such as Golden goat cheese soufflé.

INNKEEPERS:	Kris & Lynn Sheehan
ADDRESS:	6901 Freedom Boulevard
	Aptos, California 95003
TELEPHONE:	(831) 688-8005
E-MAIL:	lynn@sandrockfarm.com
WEBSITE:	www.sandrockfarm.com
ROOMS:	5 Rooms; 3 Suites; Private baths
CHILDREN:	Welcome
ANIMALS:	Not allowed; Resident cat
HANDICAPPED:	Not handicapped accessible
DIETARY NEEDS:	Will accommodate guests' special dietary needs

Goat Cheese Soufflé

Makes 12 Servings

"This soufflé is one of our most popular dishes. It is wonderful atop a seasonal salad, such as springtime asparagus tips, English peas and baby greens or sun-dried tomatoes and summer corn with romaine lettuce. In fall, try caramelized onion, diced apples and butter lettuce. In winter, try greens with balsamic vinaigrette and dried fruits." ~ Innkeeper, Sand Rock Farm Bed & Breakfast

¼	cup dry breadcrumbs
3	tablespoons butter, plus extra for buttering ramekins
3	tablespoons cake flour
1	cup milk
10	ounces goat cheese, divided
3	egg yolks

Salt and pepper, to taste
1	cup egg whites (about 7 egg whites)

Preheat oven to 425°F. Butter 12 (5-ounce) ramekins or standard muffin cups. Dust with breadcrumbs, then turn out excess breadcrumbs. Melt 3 tablespoons of butter in a saucepan over medium heat. Whisking constantly, add flour. Whisk in milk and cook for about 3 minutes, until mixture has thickened to the consistency of a thin pudding.

Crumble ¾ of goat cheese into a bowl. Pour hot milk mixture over goat cheese; mix well. Add egg yolks; mix well. Season with salt and pepper. Beat egg whites with a mixer until stiff peaks form. Fold ½ of egg whites into milk mixture, then fold in remaining egg whites. Divide ½ of milk mixture among ramekins. Crumble remaining goat cheese into ramekins, then top with remaining milk mixture. (Soufflés may be held at room temperature for up to 6 hours before baking.)

Put ramekins in a large baking pan. Add enough boiling water to baking pan to come halfway up sides of ramekins. Bake for 25 minutes, or until golden. Remove from oven and let ramekins stand in pan for 15 minutes. Using a towel to hold ramekins, run a knife around inside rim to loosen soufflés. Turn out soufflés onto serving plates to serve.

Gaige House Inn

GAIGE HOUSE INN

S et in the beautiful Sonoma Valley, this luxurious Wine Country bed & breakfast inn is a stylish getaway for those visiting the Sonoma and Napa Wine Country. The inn is just a stone's throw from winery tours, hiking and biking in the lovely Sonoma Valley. Close to all Napa Valley has to offer, this award-winning, beautifully designed inn rivals the finest California hotels.

"Chef Holmes' breakfasts venture so far from the common that most feel that they alone are worth the stay." ~ 2003 Zagat Survey

INNKEEPERS:	Ken Burnet & Greg Nemrow
ADDRESS:	13540 Arnold Drive
	Glen Ellen, California 95442
TELEPHONE:	(800) 935-0237
E-MAIL:	gaige@sprynet.com
WEBSITE:	www.gaige.com
ROOMS:	11 Rooms; 13 Suites; 4 Cottages; Private baths
CHILDREN:	Children age 16 and older welcome
ANIMALS:	Not allowed
HANDICAPPED:	Handicapped accessible
DIETARY NEEDS:	Will accommodate guests' special dietary needs

Tomato, Corn & Gruyère Galette

Makes 8 Servings

Galette dough:
1¼   cups all-purpose flour
⅓   cup fine yellow cornmeal
1   teaspoon sugar
¾   teaspoon salt
6   tablespoons unsalted butter, chilled and cut into ½-inch pieces
3   tablespoons olive oil
¼   cup ice water

Galette filling:
2   tablespoons olive oil
1   large white onion, thinly sliced
Salt and freshly ground pepper, to taste
2   cloves garlic, minced
½   cup chopped fresh basil, plus thinly sliced basil, for garnish
Corn kernels cut from 1 ear of fresh corn
2   medium tomatoes, cut into ⅓-inch-thick slices and drained
¾   cup grated Gruyère or Comte cheese
Egg wash (1 egg yolk beaten with 1 teaspoon of milk)

For the dough: In a bowl, combine flour, cornmeal, sugar and salt. Cut in butter with a mixer until butter is the size of coarse cornmeal with a few large chunks. Add olive oil and ice water; mix until dough comes together. Gather dough with your hands and form into a disk. Wrap in plastic wrap and chill for at least 2 hours.

For the filling: Preheat oven to 375°F. Heat oil in a skillet over medium heat. Add onions; cook, stirring often, until lightly browned. Season with salt and pepper. Add garlic, chopped basil and corn; cook for 1 minute, then set aside to cool. Roll dough into a 15-inch round. Transfer dough to a pizza stone or a parchment paper-lined baking sheet. Spread onion mixture over dough, leaving a 2-inch border. Put tomatoes in a single layer on top of onions. Season with salt and pepper. Sprinkle with cheese. Fold dough over filling, pleating border as you go. Brush with egg wash. Bake for about 40 minutes, until crust is browned. Garnish with sliced basil.

Tiffany House

Nestled among spreading oaks, high on a hilltop with panoramic views, sits the Tiffany House, a late Victorian two-story home. A large, shaded deck with comfortable wicker furnishings, a quaint gazebo and a relaxing hammock create a sense of nostalgia and tranquillity.

Bedrooms have queen-size beds covered in hand-crocheted bed spreads and embroidered pillow cases, down pillows and cozy robes. Each room has a view of the magnificent Mt. Lassen mountain range. The Oak Room's sitting area features a dozen, signed Wallace Nutting originals.

INNKEEPERS:	Susan & Brady Stewart
ADDRESS:	1510 Barbara Road
	Redding, California 96003
TELEPHONE:	(530) 244-3225
E-MAIL:	tiffanyhse@aol.com
WEBSITE:	www.sylvia.com/tiffany.htm
ROOMS:	4 Rooms; 1 Cottage; Private baths
CHILDREN:	Welcome
ANIMALS:	Not allowed; Resident outdoor cats
HANDICAPPED:	Handicapped accessible
DIETARY NEEDS:	Will accommodate guests' special dietary needs

Spicy Smoked Salmon Corn Cake

Makes 2 Servings

"This is adapted from Gourmet *magazine's* Quick Kitchen Cookbook. *Our guests are surprised to have salmon for breakfast. It's one of our favorite dishes."*
~ Innkeeper, Tiffany House Bed & Breakfast Inn

¼	cup plus 2 tablespoons yellow cornmeal
3	tablespoons all-purpose flour
¼	teaspoon baking soda
¼	teaspoon salt
1	large egg, lightly beaten
3	tablespoons cream cheese, softened
¼	cup plus 2 tablespoons buttermilk
½	cup fresh or frozen (thawed) corn
3	tablespoons finely chopped chives (or 1 tablespoon dried)
9	pepperoncini peppers, drained, seeded and finely chopped
3	ounces finely chopped smoked salmon (about ⅓ cup)

Sour cream, for serving
Chopped red onion, for serving
Lemon slices, for serving

In a small bowl, whisk together cornmeal, flour, baking soda and salt. In a medium bowl, whisk together egg and cream cheese. Whisk buttermilk into egg mixture.

Coarsely chop ½ of corn; stir into egg mixture along with remaining corn, chives, pepperoncini, smoked salmon and cornmeal mixture just until combined.

Drop batter by ¼-cupsful onto a large, non-stick or greased griddle or skillet; spread batter slightly to form 3½- to 4-inch cakes. Cook cakes for 2-3 minutes per side, until golden brown on both sides. Serve with sour cream, chopped red onion and lemon slices.

MacCallum House Inn

Come and enjoy the warmth and hospitality of the MacCallum House Inn, Mendocino's finest restaurant, bar and country inn. This circa 1882 Victorian mansion was built by William Kelley as a wedding gift to his daughter, Daisy MacCallum. Filled with charm, romance and antiques, the historic landmark MacCallum House stands at the very heart of the quiet village of Mendocino.

A full breakfast is served in the acclaimed restaurant and a wine hour features selections from across California's Wine Country.

INNKEEPERS:	Jed & Megan Ayres & Noah Sheppard
ADDRESS:	45020 Albion Street
	Mendocino, California 95460
TELEPHONE:	(707) 937-0289; (800) 609-0492
E-MAIL:	info@maccallumhouse.com
WEBSITE:	www.maccallumhouse.com
ROOMS:	21 Rooms; 5 Suites; 9 Cottages; Private baths
CHILDREN:	Welcome
ANIMALS:	Dogs & cats welcome
HANDICAPPED:	Handicapped accessible
DIETARY NEEDS:	Will accommodate guests' special dietary needs

Wild Mushroom Hash

Makes 8 to 10 Servings

½   pound applewood-smoked bacon, chopped into ¼-inch dice
2   pounds red potatoes, chopped into ¼-inch dice
1   medium onion, chopped into ¼-inch dice
1   pound fresh chanterelle mushrooms, chopped into ¼-inch dice
1   pound fresh porcini mushrooms, chopped into ¼-inch dice
Sea salt and freshly ground black pepper, to taste

Preheat oven to 350°F. Cook bacon in a skillet, then transfer to a bowl; reserve bacon grease. Put a light layer of reserved bacon grease in a large skillet over medium to medium-high heat; heat until grease just begins to smoke. Add just enough potatoes to cover bottom of pan. Cook potatoes, stirring occasionally, until golden and tender. Put cooked potatoes in bowl with bacon. Repeat with remaining potatoes.

Put another light layer of bacon grease in skillet over medium heat. Add onions and cook until slightly browned and soft. Add chanterelle and porcini mushrooms (reserve a few of each for garnish) and cook until tender. Add onion mixture to bacon and potatoes; mix well. Season with salt and pepper. Divide hash among plates. Garnish with reserved mushrooms to serve.

Note: The cooked hash can be covered and refrigerated for up to 48 hours. Reheat by heating a touch of bacon grease or canola oil in a skillet over medium heat. Add a thin layer of hash and heat through. For a vegetarian dish, omit the bacon and use canola oil for cooking.

Grand View Inn

The Grand View Inn is a truly romantic inn on the very edge of Monterey Bay. A comfortable feeling of quiet elegance fills the inn, reinforced by the slight sound of sea breeze that permeates the air. This is the perfect spot to relax and enjoy all the beauty nature has to offer.

The Seal Rocks Room offers a twelve-foot-wide picture window with an almost surreal view of all of Monterey Bay and the Lover's Point beach area. A crystal chandelier compliments the large armoire and the antique brass, queen-size bed with inlaid wood that is the focal point of the room.

INNKEEPERS:	Susan Wheelwright & Ed Flatley
ADDRESS:	557 Ocean View Boulevard
	Pacific Grove, California 93950
TELEPHONE:	(831) 372-4341
E-MAIL:	None available
WEBSITE:	www.pginns.com
ROOMS:	11 Rooms; 1 Suite; 1 Cottage; Private baths
CHILDREN:	Children age 12 and older welcome
ANIMALS:	Not allowed
HANDICAPPED:	Handicapped accessible
DIETARY NEEDS:	Will accommodate guests' special dietary needs

Oven-Roasted Tomatoes

Makes 8 Servings

"Slow roasting these tomatoes develops a deep, rich flavor. The balsamic vinegar adds a warm tang, and the garlic and fresh basil round out the flavors. Lovely as a breakfast side dish, these work equally well as part of a dinner menu." ~ Innkeeper, Grand View Inn

2	cups cherry tomatoes
2	cups good-sized wedges mixed yellow and orange tomatoes
8	large Roma tomatoes, quartered
3	tablespoons extra-virgin olive oil
2	tablespoons balsamic vinegar
½	teaspoon salt
½	teaspoon sugar
¼	teaspoon white pepper
6	large cloves garlic, peeled
8	large basil leaves, cut into chiffonade (long, thin strips)
1	cup breadcrumbs

Preheat oven to 350°F. Put tomatoes in a large stainless steel bowl. Add remaining ingredients, except basil and breadcrumbs; toss gently to combine. Put tomatoes in a thoroughly buttered 9x13-inch baking dish. Roast for 45-60 minutes, until tomatoes have released their juices and are very fragrant.

Remove tomatoes from oven and stir in basil (be careful – tomatoes and baking dish will be very hot). Top with breadcrumbs. Return tomatoes to oven and roast for about 20 minutes longer, until breadcrumbs are lightly toasted. Serve hot or at room temperature.

Gaige House Inn

GAIGE HOUSE INN

Breakfast at the Gaige House Inn has always been something special, but with the addition of chef Charles Holmes, it has catapulted to an experience of taste and indulgence. Chef Holmes, having worked with and been trained by such talents as Gary Danko, Phillipe Jeanty and Hugh Carpenter of Domain Chandon, conveys a fresh energy and unique style.

Chef Holmes brings the creativity usually associated with dinner to breakfast. His signature dish, artichoke and pistachio blini with home-smoked salmon, asparagus and saffron cream, is fast becoming a Gaige House favorite.

INNKEEPERS:	Ken Burnet & Greg Nemrow
ADDRESS:	13540 Arnold Drive
	Glen Ellen, California 95442
TELEPHONE:	(800) 935-0237
E-MAIL:	gaige@sprynet.com
WEBSITE:	www.gaige.com
ROOMS:	11 Rooms; 13 Suites; 4 Cottages; Private baths
CHILDREN:	Children age 16 and older welcome
ANIMALS:	Not allowed
HANDICAPPED:	Handicapped accessible
DIETARY NEEDS:	Will accommodate guests' special dietary needs

Zucchini Pancakes with Roasted Red Pepper & Crescenza Cheese

Makes 6 Servings

Bellwether Farms is an artisanal cheese maker in Northern California. Their Crescenza cheese is a buttery, soft-ripened, cow's milk cheese with a rich, slightly tart flavor. It is available at many cheese and gourmet stores, some Whole Foods and Wild Oats Markets or at www.bellwethercheese.com.

2	cups grated zucchini
¾	cup all-purpose flour

Salt and pepper, to taste

½	teaspoon nutmeg
4	large eggs
3	tablespoons butter, melted and cooled
¼	cup water
⅓	cup grated Parmesan cheese
2	ounces Bellwether Farms Crescenza cheese (or Brie)
2	cups sliced (¼-inch-thick) roasted red bell pepper

Kosher salt, to taste

Lemon juice, to taste

Extra-virgin olive oil, to taste

Chopped chives, for garnish

Put zucchini in a tea towel and squeeze out liquid. In a medium bowl, combine flour, salt, pepper and nutmeg. In a small bowl, whisk eggs. Mix butter and water into eggs; stir into flour mixture. Stir in zucchini and Parmesan cheese (if batter is too thick, add up to ¼ cup more water).

Heat a non-stick skillet over medium heat. Add batter by spoonfuls and cook for until golden brown on each side, about 2 minutes per side. Spread a little Crescenza cheese over each pancake. Sprinkle roasted red bell peppers with kosher salt, lemon juice and olive oil. Divide bell peppers among plates. Garnish with chives to serve.

The Brewery Gulch Inn

The Brewery Gulch Inn, which opened in 2001, combines yesterday's history with today's comforts. On ten acres, encompassing mature redwoods, pine trees, hundreds of rhododendrons and many native plants, the inn offers a peaceful retreat for those enjoying the North Coast's many recreational opportunities and the delights of Mendocino.

Guest rooms, most with private redwood decks, are furnished to provide ultimate comfort. Each room has an ocean view, fine linens, fireplace, luxury toiletries, robes and a cozy sitting area.

INNKEEPERS:	Mina Lev & Patty Neumier
ADDRESS:	9401 Coast Highway One North
	Mendocino, California 95460
TELEPHONE:	(707) 937-4752; (800) 578-4454
E-MAIL:	info@brewerygulchinn.com
WEBSITE:	www.brewerygulchinn.com
ROOMS:	10 Rooms; Private baths
CHILDREN:	Children age 12 and older welcome
ANIMALS:	Not allowed
HANDICAPPED:	Handicapped accessible; 1 room
DIETARY NEEDS:	Will accommodate guests' special dietary needs

Red Chile-Glazed Bacon

Makes 6 Servings

12   slices thick-cut applewood-smoked bacon
¼   cup brown sugar
Kosher salt, to taste
Freshly cracked black pepper, to taste
1   tablespoon crushed dried red chiles or red pepper flakes

Preheat oven to 350°F. Lay bacon on a parchment paper-lined baking sheet. Sprinkle with brown sugar, salt, pepper and crushed red chiles. Bake for 20 minutes. Drain and serve.

Note: This bacon will not be crisp like thin-cut bacon.

The Groveland Hotel

~1914~ ~1849~

Founded in 1849, Groveland was a rough-and-ready gold mining town at Yosemite's front door. The original adobe Groveland Hotel at Yosemite National Park was constructed around 1850. Known as "The Best House on the Hill" at the height of the Gold Rush, the Groveland Hotel is the ideal base for all sorts of recreation in the Sierra Nevada Mountains.

The Groveland Hotel Restaurant features outstanding cuisine prepared with fresh, local, seasonal ingredients. Most herbs are grown in the hotel's garden and produce comes from local farms.

INNKEEPERS:	Peggy & Grover Mosley
ADDRESS:	18767 Main Street
	Groveland, California 95321
TELEPHONE:	(209) 962-4000; (800) 273-3314
E-MAIL:	info@groveland.com
WEBSITE:	www.groveland.com
ROOMS:	14 Rooms; 3 Suites; Private baths
CHILDREN:	Welcome
ANIMALS:	Welcome; Resident dog
HANDICAPPED:	Handicapped accessible
DIETARY NEEDS:	Will accommodate guests' special dietary needs

Aunt Dora's Southern Barbecue Sauce

Makes About 16 Pints

"This recipe is from an incredible menu of Southern barbecue as it was prepared several generations ago at Leonard's Barbecue on Old Highway 51 South in Memphis, Tennessee. It was passed down to me from my aunt, Dora Simmons. As a former schoolmate and neighbor of Elvis Presley – we're all from Memphis – we enjoyed this type of food often. We treasure this recipe today and share it with our guests every summer." – Innkeeper, The Groveland Hotel at Yosemite National Park

7	cups chopped onion
1	gallon ketchup
8	cups water
2	cups chili powder
¼	cup dry mustard
2½	cups Worcestershire sauce
2	teaspoons minced garlic
1	gallon red wine vinegar
4	pounds dark brown sugar
2½	cups plus 3 tablespoons paprika
12	bay leaves
2	cups crushed red pepper flakes

Combine all ingredients in a large pot. Bring just to a boil, then immediately remove from heat (mixture will be very thin). Cool and seal in sterilized containers with tight-fitting lids. Store for 30 days to age. When ready to use, open only as much as is needed. When sauce is exposed to air, it will thicken immediately. Use on pork, chicken, beef, shrimp, etc.

Note: You can cut this recipe down, but the results may not be the same. Be sure to follow canning safety procedures.

Casa Tropicana

Overlooking the Pacific Ocean at the San Clemente Pier, the Casa Tropicana holds the promise of adventure, sun, sand and surf. With a five mile stretch of sandy beaches and vast blue ocean, you will feel you are in a secluded tropical paradise. Guest rooms carry you into a tropical paradise of your choice. Each is named for and designed in the style of a different island resort, such as Key Largo, Bali Hai and Jungle Paradise.

The Out of Africa Suite has a featherbed, fireplace, seven-foot Jacuzzi tub for two, dark woods, Oriental rugs and oak flooring.

INNKEEPERS:	Rick Anderson
ADDRESS:	610 Avenida Victoria
	San Clemente, California 92672
TELEPHONE:	(949) 492-1234; (800) 492-1245
E-MAIL:	rick@rickstropicana.com
WEBSITE:	www.casatropicana.com
ROOMS:	9 Rooms; Private baths
CHILDREN:	Welcome
ANIMALS:	Not allowed
HANDICAPPED:	Handicapped accessible
DIETARY NEEDS:	Will accommodate guests' special dietary needs

Hawaiian Teriyaki Marinade

Makes About 1 Quart

"This recipe is from a Maui native." ~ Innkeeper, Casa Tropicana

1   habanero pepper, chopped
1   large piece ginger root, peeled and chopped
1   quart Aloha soy sauce (or any low-salt soy sauce)
1   cup packed brown sugar
1   teaspoon sesame oil
1   teaspoon sesame seeds

Combine habanero pepper and ginger in a large bowl. Add remaining ingredients and stir. Use marinade with grilled chicken, beef or pork.

Appetizers, Soups & Salads

Appetizers, Soups & Salads

Collingwood Inn

The lovely, historic Collingwood Inn is a Victorian estate built in 1885. Take a stroll or relax in the gardens. Let the innkeepers provide you with a picnic basket for an afternoon in the redwoods or by the ocean. Pamper yourself with an aroma-therapy bubble bath in a claw-foot tub with inn-made bath salts and bubble-bath ingredients.

"A showpiece grand old manor with a fabulous breakfast and the full Victorian treatment." ~ *San Francisco Chronicle*

INNKEEPERS:	Chris Hanks & Peter Consello
ADDRESS:	831 Main Street
	Ferndale, California 95536
TELEPHONE:	(707) 786-9219; (800) 469-1632
E-MAIL:	innkeepers@collingwoodinn.com
WEBSITE:	www.collingwoodinn.com
ROOMS:	4 Rooms; Private baths
CHILDREN:	Children welcome
ANIMALS:	Welcome; Resident dog & wolves
HANDICAPPED:	Handicapped accessible; 1 room
DIETARY NEEDS:	Will accommodate guests' special dietary needs

Prosciutto-Wrapped Figs

Makes 24 Servings

"From grandmother in Venice." ~ Innkeeper, Collingwood Inn Bed & Breakfast

6   large fresh figs, quartered
6   thin slices prosciutto, quartered
Extra-virgin olive oil
Freshly ground pepper, to taste
1   tablespoon fresh lime juice

Preheat broiler. Roll each fig quarter tightly in a quarter slice of prosciutto and secure with a toothpick. With a pastry brush, brush each wrapped fig lightly with olive oil and grind a bit of pepper over the top.

Broil figs for about 1 minute on each side. Transfer figs to a platter and remove toothpicks. Drizzle figs with more olive oil and sprinkle with lime juice. Insert new toothpicks and serve.

Bridge Creek Inn

Nestled near the vineyards of the Edna Valley, just minutes from San Luis Obispo, the Bridge Creek Inn offers pastoral views of the Santa Lucia Mountains and a spectacular, nightly show of uncountable stars.

This custom-designed bed & breakfast sits on ten acres of gently rolling hills with a seasonal stream. Here, you can retreat from the pressures of daily life by relaxing in the outdoor spa, visiting the many nearby wineries or exploring the scenic California coast.

INNKEEPERS:	Sally & Gene Kruger
ADDRESS:	5300 Righetti Road
	San Luis Obispo, California 93401
TELEPHONE:	(805) 544-3003
E-MAIL:	info@bridgecreekinn.com
WEBSITE:	www.bridgecreekinn.com
ROOMS:	2 Rooms; Private baths
CHILDREN:	Not allowed
ANIMALS:	Not allowed
HANDICAPPED:	Not handicapped accessible
DIETARY NEEDS:	Will accommodate guests' special dietary needs

Brie with Strawberries in Puff Pastry

Makes 8 Servings

½   cup raspberry, strawberry or plum jam
¼   cup chopped strawberries
½   teaspoon chopped rosemary, plus rosemary sprigs, for garnish
1   sheet puff pastry (½ of a 17-ounce package), thawed
1   (13-ounce) wheel Brie cheese (about 6- to 7-inches in diameter)
1   egg, beaten
Grape clusters, for garnish
Baguette slices or crackers, for serving

Preheat oven to 400°F. In a small bowl, combine jam, strawberries and chopped rosemary. Roll out puff pastry slightly into a 12-inch square.

Cut rind off top of Brie. Put cheese, cut-side-up, in center of puff pastry sheet. Spread jam mixture over top of Brie. Fold puff pastry over Brie; wet edges and press to seal. Brush pastry with egg. Transfer to a baking sheet and bake for 20 minutes. Cool for 10 minutes. Garnish with rosemary sprigs and grape clusters. Serve with baguette slices or crackers.

Oak Creek Manor

The AAA Four-Diamond Oak Creek Manor is secluded on eight acres with beautiful gardens and a romantic gazebo overlooking the pond and dock. Rooms are filled with antiques from around the world, and have private patios and Jacuzzi tubs or fireplaces. A gourmet breakfast with homemade jams and baked goods guarantees a healthy start to the day. The inn uses only organic produce from local growers and farmers' markets.

"We had a truly wonderful experience – great food and wine in a beautiful setting. Our suite was outstanding." ~ Guests, Oak Creek Manor

INNKEEPERS:	Ingrid & Johannes Zachbauer
ADDRESS:	4735 Olive Hill Road
	Fallbrook, California 92028
TELEPHONE:	(760) 451-2468; (877) 451-2468
E-MAIL:	oakcreekmanor@adelphia.net
WEBSITE:	www.oakcreekmanor.com
ROOMS:	4 Rooms; 2 Suites; 1 Cottage; Private baths
CHILDREN:	Children age 14 and older welcome
ANIMALS:	Not allowed
HANDICAPPED:	Not handicapped accessible
DIETARY NEEDS:	Will accommodate guests' special dietary needs

Spinach Feta Strudel

Makes 36 Pieces

2   pounds fresh baby spinach, washed and trimmed
½   stick butter plus 2 sticks unsalted butter, melted
12   green onions (white parts only), minced (about ½ cup)
6   ounces feta cheese, chilled and coarsely chopped
½   cup fresh breadcrumbs, divided
¼   cup minced fresh parsley
4   egg whites
¼   cup minced fresh dill (or 4 teaspoons dried)
Salt and freshly ground pepper, to taste
¾   pound phyllo dough

Cook spinach briefly in a pot with just enough water to dampen leaves, turning twice to cook evenly. Once spinach wilts, transfer to a colander and run under cold water until cool. Purée spinach in a food processor; reserve spinach in food processor.

Melt ½ stick of butter in a small skillet over medium heat. Add green onions and cook for 5 minutes. Add green onions to spinach in food processor, along with feta cheese, 2 tablespoons of breadcrumbs, parsley, egg whites, dill, salt and pepper. Process well. Taste and adjust seasoning; mixture should be highly seasoned.

Preheat oven to 375°F. Butter a baking sheet. Dampen a paper towel or towel and cover with waxed paper. Place 1 sheet of phyllo on waxed paper. Brush each sheet of phyllo with melted unsalted butter and sprinkle with 1 tablespoon of breadcrumbs.

Stack phyllo sheets and spread ⅓ of spinach mixture on phyllo to within ½ inch of long edge. Roll tightly, using waxed paper to help. Transfer to baking sheet. Brush top lightly with melted unsalted butter. Repeat process 2 more times, to yield 3 phyllo rolls. Bake for 30-35 minutes, until golden brown. Cut into 1-inch-thick slices with a serrated knife and serve.

Windrose Inn

T he hospitality of a bygone era lives on in the Windorse Inn, a spacious, circa 1897 Victorian home. Nestled on a country road between the historic mining towns of Jackson and Sutter Creek, the Windrose offers elegantly appointed rooms, a full gourmet breakfast, a late afternoon wine hour and all the comforts of a quiet country home.

Windrose Inn guests greet the morning to the sounds of chirping birds while sipping freshly brewed coffee or tea in the privacy of their rooms or on the terrace overlooking the Koi pond and rose garden.

INNKEEPERS:	Paula & Bruce Stanbridge
ADDRESS:	1407 Jackson Gate Road
	Jackson, California 95642
TELEPHONE:	(209) 223-3650; (888) 568-5250
E-MAIL:	info@windroseinn.com
WEBSITE:	www.windroseinn.com
ROOMS:	3 Rooms; 1 Suite; Private baths
CHILDREN:	Welcome
ANIMALS:	Not allowed; Resident dog
HANDICAPPED:	Not handicapped accessible
DIETARY NEEDS:	Will accommodate guests' special dietary needs

Chèvre Herb Toasts with Spicy Jelly

Makes 8 Servings

"These are delightfully simple, absolutely delicious and very beautiful." ~ Innkeeper, Windrose Inn

1   sourdough baguette, sliced ½-inch thick
1   (8-ounce) log chèvre (goat cheese), sliced ¼-inch thick
2   tablespoons herbes de Provence

Spicy jelly:
⅔   cup apricot jam
⅓   cup habanero or jalapeño jelly

Preheat oven to 350°F. Lightly spray a cookie sheet with canola oil or non-stick cooking spray. Place baguette slices on cookie sheet. Bake for 10-15 minutes, until golden; set aside to cool for 5 minutes. Place 1 slice of chèvre on each baguette slice. Sprinkle with ¼ teaspoon of herbes de Provence. Bake for 3-5 minutes, until cheese is soft, but not melted. Transfer to a serving plate and place ¼-½ teaspoon of spicy jelly in center of each baguette slice. Serve immediately.

For the spicy jelly: Combine apricot jam and habanero or jalapeño jelly.

Inn at Depot Hill

Located two blocks from the beach in the Mediterranean-style village of Capitola-by-the-Sea is the award-winning Inn at Depot Hill. The inn has received the prestigious Mobil Four-Star award each year since 1997 and has been named one of the top ten inns in the country.

Appointments are rich and luxurious, and echo an opulent past. The inn's upscale rooms are named for and luxuriously decorated in the style of legendary parts of the world: the Cote d'Azur Room captures the essence of a chic auberge in St. Tropez; the Portofino Room, an Italian coastal villa.

INNKEEPERS:	Aurorah Cheney
ADDRESS:	250 Monterey Avenue
	Capitola, California 95010
TELEPHONE:	(831) 462-3376; (800) 572-2632
E-MAIL:	aurorah@innsbythesea.com
WEBSITE:	www.innsbythesea.com
ROOMS:	12 Suites; Private baths
CHILDREN:	Children age 8 and older welcome
ANIMALS:	Not allowed
HANDICAPPED:	Handicapped accessible
DIETARY NEEDS:	Will accommodate guests' special dietary needs

Asiago Cheese Dip with Beer Bread

Makes 10 to 12 Servings

Beer bread:

3   cups all-purpose flour
½   cup sugar
1   tablespoon honey, warmed slightly (aids mixing)
1   (12-ounce) bottle beer (amber or red ales work well)
1   cup grated cheese (cheddar works well)
1   tablespoon butter, melted

Preheat oven to 350°F. Combine flour and sugar. Add honey and beer; mix thoroughly. Stir in cheese. Place dough in a 9x5-inch loaf pan. Brush with melted butter. Bake for 1 hour. Cool, then slice.

Asaigo cheese dip:

2   tablespoons butter
12   mushrooms, sliced
¼   cup chopped oil-packed sun-dried tomatoes
½   cup chopped green onions
Salt and pepper, to taste
1   cup mayonnaise
1   cup sour cream
1½   cups grated Asiago cheese, divided

Preheat oven to 350°F. Melt butter in a skillet over medium heat. Add mushrooms, sun-dried tomatoes and green onions; cook until mushrooms are soft. Season with salt and pepper. Combine mayonnaise, sour cream and 1 cup of Asiago cheese. Stir in mushroom mixture until well combined. Transfer mixture to a small baking dish. Sprinkle with remaining ½ cup of Asiago cheese. Bake for 15 minutes, or until mixture is smooth and cheese topping has melted. Serve warm with beer bread.

Old World Inn

The historic, circa 1906 Old World Inn was built as a private residence. The inn has an eclectic combination of architectural styles, detailed with wood shingles, wide, shady porches, clinker brick and leaded and beveled glass windows. The inn is furnished with painted antiques. Scandinavian colors dominate the parlor which, along with its fireplace and soft classical music, is the perfect escape from the rushing world.

Guest rooms have been individually decorated with coordinated linens. Most have a Victorian claw-foot tub, and one has a private spa tub.

INNKEEPERS:	Russ Herschelmann & Sharon Fry
ADDRESS:	1301 Jefferson Street
	Napa, California 94559
TELEPHONE:	(707) 257-0112
E-MAIL:	innkeeper@oldworldinn.com
WEBSITE:	www.oldworldinn.com
ROOMS:	9 Rooms; 1 Cottage; Private baths
CHILDREN:	Welcome
ANIMALS:	Not allowed
HANDICAPPED:	Not handicapped accessible
DIETARY NEEDS:	Will accommodate guests' special dietary needs

Olive Tapenade

Makes 8 to 12 Servings

"We pair this tapenade with freshly baked bread and pita chips as part of our wine and appetizer hour – it is always a big hit. This recipe is adapted from one at the Ink House Bed & Breakfast in Napa." – Innkeeper, Old World Inn

¾	cup canned ripe black olives
1	teaspoon lemon juice
½	cup pimento-stuffed Spanish green olives
1	tablespoon capers
½	teaspoon Italian seasoning
1	teaspoon minced garlic
1½	teaspoons chopped fresh parsley
1½	tablespoons pine nuts or sunflower seeds

Dash of cayenne pepper
1   (8-ounce) package cream cheese, for serving
Sliced bread, pita chips and/or gourmet crackers, for serving

Put all ingredients, except cream cheese and bread, in a food processor and pulse for 30 seconds. Chill and serve over cream cheese with sliced bread, pita chips and/or gourmet crackers.

Haydon Street Inn

An intimate bed & breakfast, the Haydon Street Inn is located in the friendly, picturesque Sonoma Wine Country town of Healdsburg. You'll feel at home in this turn-of-the-century Queen Anne Victorian. Relax in one of the antique-furnished parlors, on the curving front porch or in the award-winning gardens. Just a short walk away is the historic town plaza with its fine boutiques, antique shops and renowned restaurants.

In addition to winery tours, guests of the inn can enjoy hot-air ballooning, bicycling or a visit to the nearby Russian River and Lake Sonoma.

INNKEEPERS:	Dick & Pat Bertapelle
ADDRESS:	321 Haydon Street
	Healdsburg, California 95448
TELEPHONE:	(707) 433-5228; (800) 528-3703
E-MAIL:	innkeeper@haydon.com
WEBSITE:	www.haydon.com
ROOMS:	8 Rooms; Private baths
CHILDREN:	Children age 12 and older welcome
ANIMALS:	Not allowed; Resident dog
HANDICAPPED:	Not handicapped accessible
DIETARY NEEDS:	Will accommodate guests' special dietary needs

Blue Cheese Appetizer

Makes 1 Cup

"Quick, easy and great at wine hour!" ~ Innkeeper, Haydon Street Inn

4   ounces blue cheese, crumbled
1   clove garlic, minced or crushed
1   medium tomato, chopped
1   tablespoon minced fresh basil (or 1 teaspoon dried)
Garlic toasts, crostini or crackers, for serving

Thoroughly combine blue cheese, garlic, tomato and basil. Serve in a decorative bowl with garlic toasts on the side.

Vagabond's House Inn

Vagabond's House
Carmel By-The-Sea, California

Nestled in the heart of the village of Carmel-By-The-Sea, near Monterey Bay, Vagabond's House Inn is a charming, brick, half-timbered English Tudor country inn. A delightful experience begins as you walk up the front steps and enter an almost magical place.

Accommodations include extraordinarily charming guest rooms with fireplaces and private baths and entrances. Vagabond's House Inn was selected as the "Best Inn on the West Coast" in 2003 by *Arrington's Bed & Breakfast Journal.*

INNKEEPERS:	Dawn Dull
ADDRESS:	4th and Dolores
	Carmel, California 93921
TELEPHONE:	(831) 624-7738; (800) 262-1262
E-MAIL:	innkeeper@vagabondshouseinn.com
WEBSITE:	www.vagabondshouseinn.com
ROOMS:	13 Rooms; Private baths
CHILDREN:	Children age 10 and older welcome
ANIMALS:	Not allowed; Resident dogs & cats
HANDICAPPED:	Not handicapped accessible
DIETARY NEEDS:	Will accommodate guests' special dietary needs

Sun-Dried Tomato Pesto Spread

Makes 6 Cups

"This spread is great on crackers or baguettes. It will keep in the refrigerator for a week or more." ~ Innkeeper, Vagabond's House Inn

3   (8-ounce) jars oil-packed sun-dried tomatoes, undrained
2   (8-ounce) packages feta cheese
⅛   teaspoon garlic salt
Oregano, to taste
1   (8-ounce) package cream cheese, softened
1   cup minced fresh parsley
⅓   cup grated Parmesan cheese
French baguette slices or crackers, for serving

Purée sun-dried tomatoes in a food processor. Crumble feta cheese into a large bowl. Add sun-dried tomatoes, garlic salt, oregano and cream cheese; mix well. Adjust seasonings to taste. Add parsley and Parmesan cheese; mix well, cover and chill. Before serving, microwave for 20-30 seconds, until spreadable. Serve with baguette slices or crackers.

Casa Laguna

Terraced on a hillside in Laguna Beach, amid tropical gardens and flower-splashed patios, the Casa Laguna Inn exudes the ambiance of bygone days when Laguna Beach was developing its reputation as an artists' colony and hideaway for Hollywood film stars.

Two lovely beaches are a few minutes walk from the inn. Located just over a mile from Main Beach, the inn is also a short distance from the many boutiques, pottery shops and galleries for which the area is famous.

INNKEEPERS:	Paul Blank & François Leclair
ADDRESS:	2510 South Coast Highway
	Laguna Beach, California 92651
TELEPHONE:	(949) 494-2996; (800) 233-0449
E-MAIL:	innkeeper@casalaguna.com
WEBSITE:	www.casalaguna.com
ROOMS:	17 Rooms; 5 Suites; 1 Cottage; Private baths
CHILDREN:	Welcome
ANIMALS:	Welcome; Resident dog
HANDICAPPED:	Not handicapped accessible
DIETARY NEEDS:	Will accommodate guests' special dietary needs

Fig & Walnut Tapenade with Goat Cheese

Makes 2 to 4 Servings

½	cup chopped, stemmed, dried Calimyma figs
3	tablespoons water
2	tablespoons chopped pitted Kalamata olives or other brine-cured black olives
1	tablespoon extra-virgin olive oil
1½	teaspoons balsamic vinegar
1½	teaspoons drained capers, chopped
¾	teaspoon chopped fresh thyme

Salt and pepper, to taste

¼	cup chopped walnuts, toasted

To serve:

1	(5½-ounce) log goat cheese
¼	cup walnut halves, toasted, for garnish

Fresh thyme sprigs, for garnish
Assorted breads, sliced and/or crackers, for serving

Combine figs and water in a small, heavy saucepan over medium-high heat; cook for about 7 minutes, until liquid evaporates and figs are soft. Transfer figs to a bowl. Mix in olives, olive oil, vinegar, capers and chopped thyme. Season with salt and pepper. Stir in chopped walnuts.

To serve: Place goat cheese log in center of a small serving dish. Arrange tapenade around goat cheese. Garnish with walnut halves and thyme sprigs. Serve with sliced bread and/or crackers.

Note: The tapenade can be prepared up to 3 days ahead, covered and refrigerated (do not add chopped walnuts if making ahead). Bring tapenade to room temperature and stir in chopped walnuts just before serving.

Ferrando's Hideaway Cottages

Ferrando's Hideaway Cottages is reminiscent of Provence in its ambiance, charm and artistic design. The cottages are just one hour from San Francisco and the Napa/Sonoma Wine Country, and just minutes from the magnificent Point Reyes National Seashore. The beauty, seclusion and exclusivity of the property sets the stage for your special moments with a special kind of luxury.

Breakfast includes a delicious array of breads, muffins, eggs from the inn's hens, yogurt, granola and seasonal berries from the inn's garden.

INNKEEPERS:	Doris & Greg Ferrando
ADDRESS:	31 Cypress Road
	Point Reyes, California 94956
TELEPHONE:	(415) 663-1966; (800) 337-2636
E-MAIL:	doris@ferrando.com
WEBSITE:	www.ferrando.com
ROOMS:	2 Cottages; Private baths
CHILDREN:	Welcome
ANIMALS:	Not allowed; Resident cat & chickens
HANDICAPPED:	Not handicapped accessible
DIETARY NEEDS:	Will accommodate guests' special dietary needs

Point Reyes Blue Spread

Makes 2 to 4 Servings

1	cup crumbled blue cheese (such as Point Reyes Blue), room temperature
1	teaspoon extra-virgin olive oil
1	tablespoon pine nuts, toasted
2	tablespoons chopped, pitted kalamata olives

Crackers or French baguette slices, for serving

Mash together blue cheese and olive oil with a fork. Fold in pine nuts and olives. Cover and refrigerate until ready to serve. Serve with crackers or baguette slices.

The Golden Gate Hotel

In 1986, the Golden Gate Hotel's owners settled down to create the kind of hotel they had always dreamed of – comfortable and charming, full of flowers and serving a great cup of coffee. Morning coffee, tea, juice and croissants are served in the downstairs parlor for a civilized start to the day.

Rooms in this circa 1913, Edwardian hotel are furnished with antiques and wicker. Some of the baths still have their original claw-foot tubs. The original birdcage elevator connects the four floors. Photos – from the historic to the absurd – line the halls, adding to the Old World ambiance.

INNKEEPERS:	John & Renate Kenaston
ADDRESS:	775 Bush Street
	San Francisco, California 94108
TELEPHONE:	(415) 392-3702; (800) 835-1118
E-MAIL:	info@goldengatehotel.com
WEBSITE:	www.goldengatehotel.com
ROOMS:	25 Rooms; Private & shared baths
CHILDREN:	Welcome
ANIMALS:	Dogs welcome; Resident cat
HANDICAPPED:	Not handicapped accessible
DIETARY NEEDS:	Will accommodate guests' special dietary needs

Grape Gazpacho

Makes 4 Servings

2	pounds seedless green grapes
1	cucumber, peeled and chopped
2	tablespoons chopped fresh dill
4	green onions, chopped
1	cup plain yogurt
2	tablespoons cream cheese, softened
2	cups half & half
¼	cup rice vinegar
2	teaspoons olive oil

Salt and white pepper, to taste
Cayenne pepper, to taste
Slivered almonds, for garnish
Chives, for garnish

Purée all ingredients, except almonds and chives, in a blender. Cover and chill thoroughly. Serve garnished with slivered almonds and chives.

Simpson House Inn

The Simpson House Inn, North America's only AAA Five-Diamond bed & breakfast inn, is secluded in an acre of English gardens, yet is only a five minute walk from Santa Barbara's restaurants, theaters, shops and museums. Mountain hikes or beach walks, in-room spa services or relaxing in the garden – invigorating or calming – the choice is yours.

"The professional service and elegant touches of an expensive hotel in a setting that allows you the illusion of weekending at a friend's posh country home." – *The Los Angeles Times*

INNKEEPERS:	The Davies Family and Janis Clapoff
ADDRESS:	121 East Arrellaga Street
	Santa Barbara, California 93101
TELEPHONE:	(805) 963-7067; (800) 676-1280
E-MAIL:	info@simpsonhouseinn.com
WEBSITE:	www.simpsonhouseinn.com
ROOMS:	8 Rooms; 4 Suites; 3 Cottages; Private baths
CHILDREN:	Welcome
ANIMALS:	Not allowed
HANDICAPPED:	Not handicapped accessible
DIETARY NEEDS:	Will accommodate guests' special dietary needs

Chilled Avocado Soup

Makes 6 Servings

4   cups chicken broth
1   onion, chopped
½   cup cream sherry
3   large ripe avocados
Salt and white pepper, to taste
1   cup heavy cream
Sour cream, for garnish
Cilantro sprigs, for garnish

Combine broth and onion in a large saucepan over high heat. Bring to a boil, lower heat and simmer for about 10 minutes. Cool mixture, then purée in a blender. Return mixture to saucepan.

Purée sherry and avocados in a blender until smooth. Transfer to a bowl and stir in whipping cream. Whisk avocado mixture into onion mixture. Season with salt and white pepper. Cover and chill. Serve with a dollop of sour cream and a cilantro sprig.

Gingerbread Cottages

Gingerbread Cottages is an enchanting property on the north shore of Clear Lake featuring intimate cottages with exquisite lakefront views. Each cottage is tastefully decorated with antiques, artwork and special attention to detail. Set on a two-acre estate, this collection of themed cottages is surrounded by large oak and bay trees.

Whether you choose water sports, a swim in the pool, enjoy the large rock barbecue surrounded by flower gardens or just sit on a private deck and listen to the splash of the water, you'll find fun and relaxation.

INNKEEPERS:	Yvonne & Buddy Lipscomb
ADDRESS:	4057 East Highway 20
	Nice, California 95464
TELEPHONE:	(707) 274-0200
E-MAIL:	mail@gingerbreadcottages.com
WEBSITE:	www.gingerbreadcottages.com
ROOMS:	10 Cottages; Private baths
CHILDREN:	Children age 12 and older welcome
ANIMALS:	Not allowed
HANDICAPPED:	Not handicapped accessible
DIETARY NEEDS:	Cannot accommodate guests' special dietary needs

Pumpkin & Shrimp Soup

Makes 2 to 4 Servings

2   tablespoons butter or margarine
2   medium white onions, sliced
2   medium carrots, thinly sliced
1   tablespoon minced cilantro
2   teaspoons grated fresh ginger
2   cloves garlic, minced
½   teaspoon allspice
1   (14-ounce) can chicken broth, divided
1   (15-ounce) can pumpkin
1   cup milk
8   ounces peeled, cooked shrimp, plus 2-4 peeled, cooked shrimp, for garnish (optional)
Plain low-fat yogurt or sour cream, for garnish (optional)
Minced fresh chives, for garnish (optional)

Melt butter in a large saucepan over medium heat. Add onions, carrots, cilantro, ginger, garlic and allspice; cook for 10-12 minutes, stirring once or twice, until vegetables are tender. Blend onion mixture and ½ cup of broth in a blender or food processor until nearly smooth.

Combine remaining broth, pumpkin and milk in saucepan used to cook onions over medium heat. Stir in onion mixture and 8 ounces of shrimp; heat through. Serve soup garnished with 1 shrimp, a dollop of yogurt or sour cream and a sprinkling of chives.

The Golden Gate Hotel

In 1986, the Golden Gate Hotel's owners settled down to create the kind of hotel they had always dreamed of – comfortable and charming, full of flowers and serving a great cup of coffee. Morning coffee, tea, juice and croissants are served in the downstairs parlor for a civilized start to the day.

Rooms in this circa 1913, Edwardian hotel are furnished with antiques and wicker. Some of the baths still have their original claw-foot tubs. The original birdcage elevator connects the four floors. Photos – from the historic to the absurd – line the halls, adding to the Old World ambiance.

INNKEEPERS:	John & Renate Kenaston
ADDRESS:	775 Bush Street
	San Francisco, California 94108
TELEPHONE:	(415) 392-3702; (800) 835-1118
E-MAIL:	info@goldengatehotel.com
WEBSITE:	www.goldengatehotel.com
ROOMS:	25 Rooms; Private & shared baths
CHILDREN:	Welcome
ANIMALS:	Dogs welcome; Resident cat
HANDICAPPED:	Not handicapped accessible
DIETARY NEEDS:	Will accommodate guests' special dietary needs

Chicken Soup with Apples & Leeks

Makes 6 Servings

1	whole chicken, cut up, washed and patted dry

Salt and pepper, to taste

½	stick butter, divided
3	leeks
2	Granny Smith apples, peeled and cut into ¼-inch cubes
3	cups chicken broth
½	cup apple cider vinegar
1	cup apple juice
3	tablespoons Calvados or other apple brandy
½	cup heavy cream

Season chicken with salt and pepper. Melt 2 tablespoons of butter in a soup pot over medium heat. Add chicken, skin-side-down, and cook for 8 minutes. Turn chicken and cook for 5 minutes longer. Remove chicken to a bowl and set aside.

Pour any butter or fat out of soup pot. Melt remaining 2 tablespoons of butter in soup pot over medium heat. Cut greens off leeks, leaving only about 1-inch of green. Slice leeks, add to pot and cook for 10 minutes, stirring occasionally, until soft, but not brown. Add chicken, apples, broth, vinegar and apple juice to leeks. Bring mixture to a slow simmer. Skim any fat. Cover pot and simmer very gently for 15 minutes, until chicken is cooked through. Remove chicken and let cool.

Skin and debone chicken. Cut meat into ½-inch chunks. Skim any fat from soup. Add Calvados and heavy cream. Bring to a simmer. Season with salt and pepper. Add chicken and simmer for 2 minutes. Serve immediately in hot bowls.

The Springville Inn

In 1911, the warm and inviting Springville Inn was built in Tule River Country to provide lodging, food and drink for travelers to the southern Sierras. The inn remains a treasured part of local history and has stood the test of time, watching over Springville for almost 100 years. The innkeepers tirelessly and lovingly restored and refurbished the inn to its past glory.

Just 17 miles northeast of Springville, Balch Park is home to some of the most beautiful and largest sequoias in the world – what John Muir called "the finest block of the big tree forest in the entire belt."

INNKEEPERS:	Carleen Kemmerling
ADDRESS:	35634 Highway 190
	Springville, California 93265
TELEPHONE:	(559) 539-7501
E-MAIL:	info@springvilleinn.com
WEBSITE:	www.springvilleinn.com
ROOMS:	8 Rooms; 2 Suites; Private baths
CHILDREN:	Children age 12 and older welcome
ANIMALS:	Not allowed
HANDICAPPED:	Handicapped accessible
DIETARY NEEDS:	Will accommodate guests' special dietary needs

Spinach Salad with Pear Nectar Vinaigrette & Candied Walnuts

Makes 4 to 6 Servings

⅓	cup white wine vinegar
⅓	cup vegetable oil
⅓	cup pear nectar
1	teaspoon Dijon mustard
¼	teaspoon salt
⅛	teaspoon pepper
12	ounces fresh baby spinach

Candied walnuts:

1	cup walnuts
½	cup sugar
2	tablespoons margarine or butter, plus extra for greasing foil

In a screw-top jar, combine vinegar, oil, pear nectar, mustard, salt and pepper. Cover and shake well to mix (can be covered and refrigerated for up to 1 week). Shake again before serving. Divide spinach among plates. Top with pear nectar vinaigrette. Sprinkle with candied walnuts.

For the candied walnuts: Line a baking sheet with foil; butter foil. Combine walnuts, sugar and 2 tablespoons of margarine or butter in a heavy, 10-inch skillet over medium heat. Cook, shaking skillet occasionally (do not stir), until sugar begins to melt. Lower heat to low and cook, stirring occasionally, until sugar is golden brown. Remove from heat and pour nuts onto a baking sheet. Cool completely, then break into clusters.

Sorensen's Resort

Nowhere in the central Sierra Nevada Mountains can you find as perfect a mountain experience as you can at Sorensen's Resort. Situated in a picturesque alpine valley ringed by aspens and stunning peaks, the resort offers almost endless possibilities year-round. Best of all, Lake Tahoe and all its attractions are just 20 minutes away.

Sorensen's Resort offers an array of workshops and activities throughout the year, with topics including stargazing, watercolor painting, music, history, holiday decorating, photography and more.

INNKEEPERS:	John & Patty Brissenden
ADDRESS:	14255 Highway 88
	Hope Valley, California 96120
TELEPHONE:	(800) 423-9949
E-MAIL:	info@sorensensresort.com
WEBSITE:	www.sorensensresort.com
ROOMS:	33 Cottages; Private & shared baths
CHILDREN:	Welcome
ANIMALS:	Dogs welcome
HANDICAPPED:	Handicapped accessible
DIETARY NEEDS:	Will accommodate guests' special dietary needs

Fresh Basil Vinaigrette

Makes About 2 Cups

"This homemade dressing has been our café's house dressing for over 20 years."
~ Innkeeper, Sorensen's Resort

½	bunch fresh basil, leaves only
2	cloves garlic, chopped
⅛	teaspoon salt
⅛	teaspoon celery salt
1¾	cups extra-virgin olive oil
½	cup red wine vinegar
1-2	dashes Worcestershire sauce
1	tablespoon stone-ground mustard
1½	teaspoons honey

In a blender, blend basil, garlic, salt and celery salt. With blender running, drizzle in olive oil. Add vinegar, Worcestershire sauce, mustard and honey; mix thoroughly, chill and serve.

Luncheon & Dinner Entrées

Luncheon

&

Dinner

Entrées

Apple Lane Inn

Aptos, California

T he Apple Lane Inn Bed & Breakfast is a large, warm 1870 Victorian farmhouse overlooking two acres of farmland, meadows, gardens and redwood groves. Explore nearby beaches, shops, restaurants, redwood forests and wineries. Sail in beautiful Monterey Bay. Visit Santa Cruz and its famous boardwalk. Look for antiques in nearby Aptos, Soquel and Capitola. With so much to see and do, you will not leave any time soon.

Relax in the Grand Parlor in front of a roaring fire and listen to the inn's player piano or browse the diverse library of movies and books.

INNKEEPERS:	Trent & Diane Wong
ADDRESS:	6265 Soquel Drive
	Aptos, California 95003
TELEPHONE:	(831) 475-6868; (800) 649-8988
E-MAIL:	info@applelaneinn.com
WEBSITE:	www.applelaneinn.com
ROOMS:	3 Rooms; 5 Suites; Private baths
CHILDREN:	Welcome
ANIMALS:	Dogs & cats welcome; Resident cats & farm animals
HANDICAPPED:	Handicapped accessible
DIETARY NEEDS:	Will accommodate guests' special dietary needs

Alder-Roasted Salmon with Shrimp & Roasted Red Pepper Mousse

Makes 6 Servings

1   head roasted garlic*
10   ounces cooked shrimp meat (about 15 medium shrimp, peeled)
¼   cup heavy cream
Basil-infused olive oil
15   fresh basil leaves, chopped plus 30 whole fresh basil leaves, divided
Juice from ½ lemon
1   egg
¼   teaspoon sugar
2   tablespoons diced roasted red pepper
Unsalted butter
6   (6-ounce) center-cut salmon filets, skin removed and divided
Salt and pepper, to taste

Squeeze roasted garlic cloves into a bowl and mash into a paste. Put garlic, shrimp, cream, 1 teaspoon of basil-infused olive oil, chopped basil leaves, lemon juice, egg and sugar in a food processor. Purée for 1-2 minutes into a mousse; transfer to a chilled metal bowl. Fold in red peppers. Season with salt and pepper. (Can be prepared up to a day in advance and refrigerated.)

Spread a generous amount of red bell pepper mousse over each of 3 salmon filets. Sandwich with remaining salmon. Brush with basil-infused olive oil. Sprinkle with salt and pepper. Preheat oven to 375°F. Prepare alder plank according to package directions, brushing plank with basil-infused olive oil. Put plank on a baking sheet. Make 3 beds of 3-4 basil leaves on plank. Sprinkle with basil-infused olive. In a skillet over medium-high heat, sear salmon for 1 minute per side. Put salmon on basil leaf beds. Top each salmon filet with 3 basil leaves. Cover with foil and roast for 9-10 minutes. Remove salmon from oven. Let rest for 2 minutes, then remove foil. Remove salmon and basil beds to plates. Garnish with fresh basil leaves to serve.

*Note: To roast garlic, cut top off garlic bulb so tops of cloves are exposed. Drizzle with basil-infused olive oil. Cover with foil and roast in a preheated 300°F oven for 1 hour, until garlic cloves are soft.

MacCallum House Inn

The MacCallum House Inn also includes the MacCallum Suites, a four-star, luxury mansion on the highest hill in Mendocino, overlooking the ocean. An easy stroll from either property brings you to untouched beaches, art galleries, live theater, shops, restaurants and rugged ocean cliffs.

The MacCallum House provides an extraordinary breakfast experience. Relax with the morning paper in the formal dining rooms next to the wood burning fireplaces, then dine in the ocean-view café or, weather permitting, outside on the wraparound sun porch.

INNKEEPERS:	Jed & Megan Ayres & Noah Sheppard
ADDRESS:	45020 Albion Street
	Mendocino, California 95460
TELEPHONE:	(707) 937-0289; (800) 609-0492
E-MAIL:	info@maccallumhouse.com
WEBSITE:	www.maccallumhouse.com
ROOMS:	21 Rooms; 5 Suites; 9 Cottages; Private baths
CHILDREN:	Welcome
ANIMALS:	Dogs & cats welcome
HANDICAPPED:	Handicapped accessible
DIETARY NEEDS:	Will accommodate guests' special dietary needs

Caramelized Day Boat Scallops with Verjus Vanilla Beurre Blanc

Makes 6 Servings

Caramelized day boat scallops:
2   pounds fresh day boat scallops
Salt

Verjus vanilla beurre blanc:
1½   sticks unsalted butter, divided
½   vanilla bean, split
2   tablespoons finely diced shallot
¼   teaspoon saffron
½   cup Navarro Vineyards verjus*
2   tablespoons heavy cream
Salt and white pepper, to taste

For the scallops: Sprinkle scallops with salt. Sear in a hot (almost smoking) skillet until golden brown on each side, about 2 minutes per side. Serve with verjus vanilla beurre blanc.

For the verjus vanilla beurre blanc: Melt 1 tablespoon of butter in a small, non-reactive saucepan (Calphalon or stainless steel) over very low heat. Scrape seeds from vanilla bean into butter along with shallots, vanilla bean pod and saffron; cook for 1 minute. Add verjus, raise heat to medium and cook until liquid is reduced by half (to about ¼ cup of liquid). Lower heat to low. Cut remaining butter into small pieces and whisk into sauce. When butter has just completely melted, immediately remove from heat and strain through a fine sieve. Whisk in cream. Season with salt and white pepper. Use immediately or hold in a prewarmed thermos for up to 1 hour.

*Note: Verjus is the non-fermented juice from unripe green grapes. It has a high acidity and a tart, apple-like flavor. In the Middle Ages, verjus was often used instead of vinegar sauces and dressings. It is available from www.navarrowine.com.

DeHaven Valley Farm

DeHaven Valley Farm & Country Inn was built in 1875 as a sheep and cattle ranch. The Manor House still stands, surrounded by 20 acres of flower-carpeted meadows, rolling coastal hills, a meandering creek and the Pacific Ocean. In 1941, DeHaven became a bed & breakfast and has been hosting guests ever since. The inn's restaurant serves fabulous four-course dinners on Wednesday through Sunday nights.

The two mile long Westport-Union Beach Landing is right across from the inn and offers spectacular surf fishing, abalone diving and whale watching.

INNKEEPERS:	R. Michael McDonald & Bill Lee-Sammons
ADDRESS:	39247 North Highway One
	Westport, California 95488
TELEPHONE:	(707) 961-1660; (877) 334-2836
E-MAIL:	info@dehavenvalleyfarm.com
WEBSITE:	www.dehavenvalleyfarm.com
ROOMS:	6 Rooms; 3 Cottages; Private & shared baths
CHILDREN:	Welcome
ANIMALS:	Welcome in cottages; Call ahead
HANDICAPPED:	Not handicapped accessible
DIETARY NEEDS:	Will accommodate guests' special dietary needs

Roast Beef Tenderloin with Mushroom Cabernet Sauce

Makes 4 to 6 Servings

Serve with Potato Cake with Bacon & Blue Cheese (see recipe on page 169).

2	tablespoons olive oil
1½	teaspoons kosher salt
1	teaspoon pepper
1	filet of beef (about 3 pounds), well trimmed and tied

Mushroom Cabernet sauce:

1	medium onion, chopped
1	tart green apple, chopped
1	carrot, peeled and chopped
2	ribs celery, chopped
2	cloves garlic, minced
1	(750-ml.) bottle Cabernet Sauvignon wine
1	cup ruby port wine
1	cup beef stock or broth
5	tablespoons butter
1	pound wild mushrooms
2	tablespoons chopped shallots

Preheat oven to 350°F. Combine oil, salt and black pepper; rub over beef. Place beef in a roasting pan and roast until a meat thermometer inserted in thickest part reads 120°F for rare (about 20 minutes) or 125-130°F for medium-rare (about 30 minutes). Cover roast loosely with foil and let stand. When ready to serve, slice roast and spoon sauce over it.

For the sauce: Heat oil in a large saucepan over medium heat. Add onion, apple, carrot, celery and garlic; cook until softened. Add wine and bring to a boil. Add port and beef stock; simmer until reduced by ⅓. Whisk in butter until melted and combined. Stir in mushrooms and shallots; cook for 1-2 minutes to marry flavors.

Sorensen's Resort

S orensen's is a historic resort in the Sierra Nevada and committed to providing hospitality, lodging and cuisine of the highest quality. Come hike, fish, ski, bike, raft, celebrate a wedding or anniversary or, as the resort's guests have been doing since 1926, simply refresh yourselves in the pure mountain air.

Choose from cozy cottages to fully outfitted log cabins and mountain homes. All are situated on the edge of Hope Valley, an incomparably scenic alpine setting ringed by aspens and criss-crossed by trout-filled rivers.

INNKEEPERS:	John & Patty Brissenden
ADDRESS:	14255 Highway 88
	Hope Valley, California 96120
TELEPHONE:	(800) 423-9949
E-MAIL:	info@sorensensresort.com
WEBSITE:	www.sorensensresort.com
ROOMS:	33 Cottages; Private & shared baths
CHILDREN:	Welcome
ANIMALS:	Dogs welcome
HANDICAPPED:	Handicapped accessible
DIETARY NEEDS:	Will accommodate guests' special dietary needs

Classic Beef Burgundy Stew

Makes 8 to 10 Servings

"This hearty stew has been our signature dish for over 20 years. It is a tasty recipe for any season. The beef is sautéed in garlic, then simmered with fresh vegetables in a rich Burgundy wine sauce." ~ Innkeeper, Sorensen's Resort

½	stick butter or margarine
5-6	cloves garlic
Pepper, to taste	
3	pounds stew meat, fat trimmed and cut into bite-size pieces
3	cups red Burgundy wine
1	tablespoon beef base or bouillon
3	cups beef consommé or broth
½	large onion, cubed
2	ribs celery, sliced
1½	tablespoons dry parsley
2	tablespoons dried basil
2	bay leaves
Garlic salt, to taste	
3-4	carrots, peeled and sliced diagonally
6	red potatoes, peeled and chopped into bite-size pieces
5-6	mushrooms, sliced
2	tablespoons cornstarch

Melt butter in a large skillet over medium heat. Add garlic and pepper. Add beef in batches and brown thoroughly. Put beef into a soup pot with wine, beef base, consommé, onion, celery, parsley, basil, bay leaves and garlic salt. Bring to a boil, lower heat, cover and simmer for 45-60 minutes, until meat is tender.

Add carrots and potatoes; simmer until tender. Add mushrooms. Adjust seasonings, to taste. To thicken, mix cornstarch with enough water to form a smooth, slightly thick mixture; stir into stew, remove from heat and serve.

The Historic National Hotel

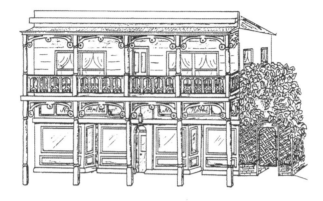

The Historic National Hotel's resident ghost, Flo, is a friendly ghost known for harmless pranks and mysterious goings on. Innkeeper Stephen Willey has been hearing stories of her presence for 28 years. Flo generally stays upstairs, seeming to favor the rooms in the front of the building, though she has on occasion been seen downstairs early in the morning, floating through the dining room and right through the walls.

"One of the best dining experiences we've ever had. We look forward to dining here again!" ~ Guests, San Francisco, California

INNKEEPERS:	Stephen Wiley
ADDRESS:	18183 Main Street
	Jamestown, California 95327
TELEPHONE:	(209) 984-3446; (800) 894-3446
E-MAIL:	info@national-hotel.com
WEBSITE:	www.national-hotel.com
ROOMS:	9 Rooms; Private baths
CHILDREN:	Children age 10 and older welcome
ANIMALS:	Dogs & cats welcome
HANDICAPPED:	Not handicapped accessible
DIETARY NEEDS:	Will accommodate guests' special dietary needs

Loin of Pork Madagascar

Makes 4 to 5 Servings

2	tablespoons olive oil or butter
1½	pounds boneless pork loin, sliced into ¼-inch medallions
	All-purpose flour
1	tablespoon chopped shallot
2	tablespoons Madagascar (green) peppercorns
¼	cup brandy
½	cup heavy cream
¼	cup plus 2 tablespoons beef stock reduction (or beef gravy)
1	tablespoon Dijon mustard
½	stick butter, softened
1	pinch ground coriander

Watercress, for garnish
Thinly sliced red bell pepper, for garnish

Flatten pork medallions between sheets of waxed paper with a mallet or the back of a heavy skillet. Heat oil or butter in a skillet over medium heat. Dredge pork in flour and add to skillet. Evenly brown both sides of each pork medallion. Add shallots and peppercorns; cook until shallots are soft.

Add brandy. Carefully light brandy with a long match; cook off alcohol. Add cream and cook until reduced slightly. Stir in beef stock reduction. Stir in mustard, butter and coriander; cook until butter is melted and combined. Remove meat to a serving platter. Reduce sauce to desired consistency. Pour sauce over meat. Garnish with watercress and red bell peppers to serve.

Dorrington Hotel & Restaurant

The circa 1852 Dorrington Hotel was originally a stagecoach stop on the Big Trees Carson Valley Road. The hotel has since been restored to provide gracious and relaxed accommodations. Brass beds, cozy homemade quilts and handsome antiques fill the comfortable, elegant rooms. Fresh fruit is always available and other amenities will make you feel at home. In the morning, a continental breakfast and a newspaper arrives at your door.

Located at 5,000 feet in the Sierra Gold Country, the Dorrington Hotel is a perfect base for exploring the many nearby attractions and activities.

INNKEEPERS:	Bonnie Saville
ADDRESS:	3431 Highway 4
	Dorrington, California 95223
TELEPHONE:	(866) 995-5800
E-MAIL:	info@dorringtonhotel.com
WEBSITE:	www.dorringtonhotel.com
ROOMS:	5 Rooms; 1 Cottage; Private & shared baths
CHILDREN:	Welcome
ANIMALS:	Not allowed
HANDICAPPED:	Not handicapped accessible
DIETARY NEEDS:	Will accommodate guests' special dietary needs

Sicilian-Style Rabbit with Artichoke Hearts

Makes 4 Servings

¼	cup olive oil
2	pounds rabbit (hindquarters work well)

All-purpose flour

12	artichoke heart quarters

Juice of 2 lemons

2	cups chicken or veal stock, plus more if needed
1	cup white wine
12	whole cloves garlic, plus 2 cloves garlic, minced

Leaves from 20 sprigs of parsley, coarsely chopped

Heat oil in a large, deep skillet over medium heat. Dredge rabbit in flour, add to skillet and brown on all sides. Add artichoke hearts, lemon juice, chicken stock, wine and whole garlic cloves. Bring to a boil. Cover, lower heat and simmer for 75 minutes, adding more stock, if needed. Stir in minced garlic and parsley to serve.

*Note: If rabbit is not available, you can substitute chicken.

Stanford Inn by the Sea

The Ravens, the Stanford Inn's vegetarian restaurant, features exceptional vegetarian and vegan cuisine. The innkeepers recognize that most of their guests are not vegetarians and have been challenged to produce satisfying and delicious meals for them. Selections including pizzas, salads, soups, elegant entrées and wonderful deserts will please any diner.

"Owners Joan and Jeff Stanford have created the ultimate escape – an inn so peaceful and so all-encompassing that there's little reason to move from the inn all weekend." ~ *Sacramento Magazine*

INNKEEPERS:	Joan & Jeff Stanford
ADDRESS:	44850 Comptche Ukiah Road
	Mendocino, California 95460
TELEPHONE:	(707) 937-5615; (800) 331-8884
E-MAIL:	stanford@stanfordinn.com
WEBSITE:	www.stanfordinn.com
ROOMS:	32 Rooms; 9 Suites; Private baths
CHILDREN:	Welcome
ANIMALS:	Welcome; Resident dogs, cats, llamas & horses
HANDICAPPED:	Handicapped accessible
DIETARY NEEDS:	Will accommodate guests' special dietary needs

Tofu Satay with Peanut Sauce

Makes 3 to 4 Servings

"This recipe is a very popular entrée or appetizer in our restaurant, the Ravens. The tofu is skewered and grilled, then served with a Thai-style peanut sauce." - Innkeeper, Stanford Inn By the Sea

1   (16-ounce) block firm teriyaki tofu

Peanut sauce:
1   tablespoon canola oil
½   cup sliced red onion
1½   teaspoons minced fresh ginger
1½   teaspoons minced garlic
2   teaspoons red chile paste
¼   cup rice vinegar
1   tablespoon white sugar
3   tablespoons brown sugar
1   tablespoon tamari soy sauce
Salt, to taste
Juice of 1 lime
¼   cup chopped cilantro leaves
½   cup coconut milk
¾   cup crunchy peanut butter

Cut tofu into 3 lengthwise slices. Grill tofu, with enough heat to leave grill marks, until crisp. Remove from heat and cut into long, wide strips. Skewer on skewers and serve with peanut sauce.

For the peanut sauce: Heat oil in a large skillet over medium heat. Add onion and ginger; cook, stirring frequently, until browned. Add garlic and chile paste; brown lightly. Add rice vinegar, white and brown sugar, tamari, salt, lime juice and cilantro. Bring to a boil. Add coconut milk and return to a boil. Purée in a blender or food processor. Return to heat and bring to a simmer. Slowly whisk in peanut butter until melted and combined.

The Springville Inn

Located in the heart of Springville and nestled in the foothills of the Sierra Nevada Mountains, the Springville Inn has dutifully stood guard at the entrance of the Giant Sequoia National Monument since 1912. Just a few hours from Los Angeles, San Francisco and the coast, the inn is the perfect weekend getaway.

The Springville Inn embodies California country casual style. Rooms and suites are filled with Western pine furnishings, quilts and ceiling fans. A delicious continental breakfast is served each day.

INNKEEPERS:	Carleen Kemmerling
ADDRESS:	35634 Highway 190
	Springville, California 93265
TELEPHONE:	(559) 539-7501
E-MAIL:	info@springvilleinn.com
WEBSITE:	www.springvilleinn.com
ROOMS:	8 Rooms; 2 Suites; Private baths
CHILDREN:	Children age 12 and older welcome
ANIMALS:	Not allowed
HANDICAPPED:	Handicapped accessible
DIETARY NEEDS:	Will accommodate guests' special dietary needs

Chicken Belle-Helene

Makes 4 Servings

Plan ahead – this dish needs to be started the night before.

4	(8-ounce) chicken breasts
1½	cups port wine, divided
¾	cup plus 3 tablespoons extra-virgin olive oil, divided
2	pears, halved or 4 canned pear halves in light syrup
8	ounces mushrooms, sliced
12	ounces fresh spinach
1½	cups chicken demi-glace*

Put chicken in a glass baking dish. Combine 1 cup of port and ¾ cup of olive oil; pour over chicken. Cover and refrigerate overnight.

The next day, preheat oven to 375°F. Remove chicken; discard marinade. Heat 2 tablespoons of olive oil in an oven-proof skillet over medium-high heat. Add chicken and brown first side. Turn chicken. Add pears and ¼ cup of Port. Transfer skillet to oven and bake for about 25 minutes, until chicken is done. Remove chicken from oven and add demi-glace and remaining ¼ cup of port; cook over medium heat for 3 minutes.

Heat remaining 1 tablespoon of olive oil in a skillet over medium heat. Add mushrooms and cook for about 2 minutes, until soft; remove and set aside. Add spinach and cook until wilted. Divide spinach between plates. Top with 1 chicken breast and sprinkle with mushrooms. Put 1 pear half to the side. Spoon pan sauce over chicken and serve.

*Note: Demi-glace is an intensely flavored stock base used to make sauces. It is often found frozen or in condensed form. If using condensed, dilute according to package directions to make needed amount.

Historic Requa Inn

The Historic Requa Inn is located on the Northern California coast, in the center of Redwood National Park on the Klamath River and just a mile from the ocean. A hotel has been operating almost continuously on this site since the 1880s. Today's Requa Inn combines the friendliness and comfort of a casual bed & breakfast with the privacy and personal service of a small hotel. It is a quiet, cozy base for your redwood adventures.

Breakfast and dinner, like the inn, are substantial and without a lot of frills. The focus is on fresh ingredients – local when possible – simply prepared.

INNKEEPERS:	David & Barbara Gross
ADDRESS:	451 Requa Road
	Klamath, California 95548
TELEPHONE:	(707) 482-1425; (866) 800-8777
E-MAIL:	innkeeper@requainn.com
WEBSITE:	www.requainn.com
ROOMS:	12 Rooms; Private baths
CHILDREN:	Children age 8 and older welcome
ANIMALS:	Not allowed; Resident dog & cat
HANDICAPPED:	Not handicapped accessible
DIETARY NEEDS:	Will accommodate guests' special dietary needs

Lemon Linguine

"With its intense lemony flavor, this pasta makes a nice side dish with fish or chicken. Or, serve it as an entrée, either as a vegetarian or topped with grilled prawns." ~ Innkeeper, Historic Requa Inn

⅔   cup heavy cream
2   egg yolks
½   cup grated Parmesan cheese
Juice and grated zest of 2 lemons (a generous ¼ cup of juice)
1   pound linguine
½   stick butter
¼   cup chopped fresh parsley

Heat cream just to the boiling point in a small, heavy saucepan over medium-high heat; remove from heat. In a small bowl, whisk egg yolks. Add hot cream, a dribble at a time, being careful not to curdle egg yolks. Stir in Parmesan cheese, lemon juice and lemon zest; set aside.

Cook pasta al dente. Melt butter in a large saucepan over medium heat. Add pasta and toss to coat. Add lemon mixture and toss to combine. Cook for about 1 minute, just to marry ingredients. Remove from heat. Add parsley, toss and serve.

The Ballard Inn

Located in the Santa Ynez Valley about 40 minutes from Santa Barbara, the Ballard Inn offers comfortably elegant accommodations in a peaceful and quiet setting in the heart of Santa Barbara Wine Country

The inn's restaurant, Cafe Chardonnay, serves creative Wine Country cuisine in a relaxed and elegant setting, paired with award-winning vintages from local wineries. Seasonal offerings might include roasted and grilled prime rib of pork with dried cherries and port wine sauce; grilled scallops wrapped in prosciutto with balsamic vinegar reduction; and chocolate mocha mousse.

INNKEEPERS:	Christine Forsyth
ADDRESS:	2436 Baseline Avenue
	Ballard, California 93463
TELEPHONE:	(805) 688-7770; (800) 638-2466
E-MAIL:	innkeeper@ballardinn.com
WEBSITE:	www.ballardinn.com
ROOMS:	15 Rooms; Private baths
CHILDREN:	Children age 12 and older welcome
ANIMALS:	Not allowed
HANDICAPPED:	Handicapped accessible
DIETARY NEEDS:	Will accommodate guests' special dietary needs

Pan-Seared Duck Breasts with Cherry Pinot Noir Sauce

Makes 4 Servings

For the duck:

4   duck breast halves (8- to 9-ounces each)
4   sprigs thyme
2   cloves garlic, chopped

For the cherry Pinot Noir sauce:

3   tablespoons dried cherries
1   tablespoon raisins
3   tablespoons brandy
2   shallots, minced
2   cloves garlic, minced
1   tablespoon butter
1   cup Pinot Noir wine
¼   cup balsamic vinegar
1   cup chicken stock
1   cup beef stock
1   tablespoon butter

For the duck: Score skin of duck in a crosshatch pattern. Trim excess fat. Rub duck with thyme and garlic. Cover and refrigerate overnight. The next day, preheat oven to 400°F. Sear duck, skin-side-down, in an oven-proof skillet over medium-high heat, until some fat is rendered and skin is golden brown. Turn duck and transfer skillet to oven. Roast duck for 8 minutes for medium-rare, or to desired doneness. Remove from oven and let rest for 5 minutes. Serve with cherry Pinot Noir sauce.

For the sauce: Soak cherries and raisins in brandy until plump. Strain; reserve brandy. Melt butter in a skillet over medium heat. Add garlic and shallots; cook until shallots are softened. Add cherries and raisins. Deglaze pan with reserved brandy. Reduce until nearly dry. Add wine; reduce until nearly dry. Add vinegar; reduce to a syrup. Add chicken and beef stocks; reduce until sauce thickens enough to coat the back of a spoon. Stir in butter until melted and combined. Season with salt and pepper.

Fruit Specialties & Desserts

Fruit Specialties & Desserts

Old St. Angela Inn

S ince 1850, Pacific Grove has maintained its quiet comfort and charm. The town lives up to its reputation as "the heart of the Monterey Peninsula." People come from all over the world to smell the sea air, explore the spectacular rocky shore and walk along cypress tree-lined trails.

Guests of the Old St. Angela Inn can enjoy nearby parks and playgrounds, gourmet dining, unique shops and galleries, scuba diving, kayaking, golf, surfing, biking, sailing and strolling along the Shoreline Recreation Trail.

INNKEEPERS:	Sue Kuslis & Lew Shaefer
ADDRESS:	321 Central Avenue
	Pacific Grove, California 93950
TELEPHONE:	(831) 372-3246; (800) 748-6306
E-MAIL:	lew@redshift.com
WEBSITE:	www.sueandlewinns.com
ROOMS:	9 Rooms; Private baths
CHILDREN:	Children age 6 and older welcome
ANIMALS:	Not allowed
HANDICAPPED:	Handicapped accessible
DIETARY NEEDS:	Will accommodate guests' special dietary needs

Fall Pear Galette

Makes 8 Servings

"This is a free-form tart featuring pears, cheddar cheese and caramel. The galette can be made a day ahead, but the caramel should be drizzled over the galette just an hour or two before it is served." ~ Innkeeper, Old St. Angela Inn

½   (15-ounce) package refrigerated pie dough (such as Pillsbury)
½   cup grated aged sharp cheddar cheese
5   ripe Bartlett or D'Anjou pears, peeled and cut into 1-inch slices
1   tablespoon lemon juice
⅛   teaspoon nutmeg
¼   cup packed brown sugar
3   tablespoons all-purpose flour

Caramel:
⅓   cup sugar

Preheat oven to 400°F. Line a jelly roll pan with foil. Coat foil with non-stick cooking spray. Roll out pie dough into an 11-inch circle and place on foil in pan. Sprinkle dough with cheese, leaving a 1-inch border. Cut pear slices in half lengthwise. Add lemon juice and nutmeg; toss to combine. Add brown sugar and flour; toss gently.

Arrange pears on dough, leaving a 2-inch border (pears will be piled high). Fold edges of dough toward center, pressing gently to seal (dough will only partially cover pears). Bake for 30 minutes, or until crust is lightly browned (filling may leak slightly during cooking). Cool galette on a wire rack.

For the caramel: Heat sugar in a small, heavy saucepan over medium heat, stirring constantly, until it dissolves, about 4 minutes. Cook for 1 minute longer, or until golden. Remove from heat and drizzle over galette.

CasaLana

CasaLana Bed & Breakfast and Gourmet Retreats is located in the charming, quaint town of Calistoga, at the top of the Napa Valley. The secluded, private setting makes it seem as if you are miles from everything, when really you're just a few blocks from Calistoga's picturesque downtown, with its numerous spas, shopping and world-class restaurants.

CasaLana offers "gourmet retreats" for home cooks and food enthusiasts. Classes are taught in the inn's professionally-equipped kitchen and range in length from a three-hour class to a five-day Culinary Learning Vacation.

INNKEEPERS:	Lana Richardson
ADDRESS:	1316 South Oak Street
	Calistoga, California 94515
TELEPHONE:	(707) 942-0615; (877) 968-2665
E-MAIL:	lana@casalana.com
WEBSITE:	www.casalana.com
ROOMS:	2 Rooms; Private baths
CHILDREN:	Welcome
ANIMALS:	Not allowed
HANDICAPPED:	Not handicapped accessible
DIETARY NEEDS:	Will accommodate guests' special dietary needs

Spiced Fruit Crostata with Preserves

Makes 8 Servings

2-3 apples (can use pears, peaches, apricots, etc.), sliced
1-2 tablespoons white sugar, depending on sweetness of fruit
1-2 tablespoons brown sugar, depending on sweetness of fruit
1 teaspoon finely chopped candied ginger
½ teaspoon cinnamon
1-2 tablespoons all-purpose flour
Finely chopped lemon, orange or lime zest, to taste
½ cup preserves, such as fig, or marmalade
1-2 tablespoons Amaretto liqueur
Pie dough (homemade or store-bought) for 1 pie
Melted unsalted butter or egg wash (1 egg beaten with 1 tablespoon of milk)
Coarse (decorating) sugar

Preheat oven to 400°F. Put apples in a large bowl. In a small bowl, combine white and brown sugar and candied ginger. Sprinkle ⅔ of sugar mixture and cinnamon over apples; toss well to coat. Let stand for a few minutes until apples give off some of their juices. Using a sieve, sprinkle flour over apples; toss well to coat. Add lemon, orange or lime zest.

Put preserves in a small saucepan over low heat and warm slightly. Add enough Amaretto to make a spreadable, but not runny mixture. Simmer for 1-2 minutes, just until well mixed. Remove from heat and cool.

Roll out dough into a ⅛-inch-thick, 12-inch disk. Transfer to a parchment paper-lined rimmed baking sheet. Spread preserve mixture over dough. Sprinkle dough with ½ of remaining sugar mixture. Arrange apples slices over dough, leaving a 2-inch border around edges. Fold the 2-inch border over apples to create a rim to seal in fruit and juice (make sure there are no cracks for juices to escape during baking).

Brush crust with melted butter or egg wash. Sprinkle crust and exposed fruit with remaining sugar mixture. Sprinkle coarse sugar over crust. Bake for 30-40 minutes, until crust is golden brown and fruit is bubbly, rotating as needed to brown crust evenly. Remove crostata from oven and transfer to a wire rack. Dab pan juice over fruit to glaze. Serve warm.

Carter House Inns

The Carter House Inns, an enclave of four magnificent Victorians perched alongside Humboldt Bay in Old Town Eureka, is consistently ranked as one of Northern California's top inns. Luxurious accommodations and sumptuous dining at the inn's Restaurant 301 (also considered among Northern California's best) set an indulgent tone for a getaway.

The innkeepers' passion for using only the freshest produce led them to start their own organic gardens. Today, the Carter House maintains the most extensive kitchen gardens of any inn on the West Coast.

INNKEEPERS:	Mark & Christi Carter
ADDRESS:	301 L Street
	Eureka, California 95501
TELEPHONE:	(707) 444-8062
E-MAIL:	reserve@carterhouse.com
WEBSITE:	www.carterhouse.com
ROOMS:	22 Rooms; 8 Suites; 2 Cottages; Private baths
CHILDREN:	Welcome
ANIMALS:	Not allowed
HANDICAPPED:	Handicapped accessible
DIETARY NEEDS:	Will accommodate guests' special dietary needs

Apple Almond Tart

Makes 8 Servings

"This recipe is adapted from one in the October 1988 Gourmet *magazine. One taste will reveal why this is our most popular recipe." ~ Innkeeper, Carter House Inns*

Crust:
1¼   cups all-purpose flour
1   stick unsalted butter, cut into pieces
2   tablespoons sugar
1   large egg

Almond filling:
⅔   cup sliced almonds, lightly toasted
½   cup sugar
2   tablespoons unsalted butter
1   large egg

Topping:
1   large Granny Smith apple, peeled and very thinly sliced
⅓   cup apricot jam, heated and strained
2   tablespoons Triple Sec or other orange-flavored liqueur

For the crust: In a food processor, process flour, butter and sugar until mixture resembles a coarse meal. Add egg and process until a soft dough is formed. On a lightly floured surface, roll out dough into an 11-inch circle. Fit dough carefully into a 9-inch tart pan with a removable fluted rim.

For the almond filling: Preheat oven to 375°F. In a food processor, finely grind almonds and sugar. Add butter and egg; process until smooth. Spread almond mixture over crust.

For the topping: Arrange apple slices on top of almond mixture. Bake tart in middle rack of oven for 25-30 minutes, or until crust is golden brown. Transfer tart to a wire rack and let cool. In a small bowl, whisk together jam and Triple Sec. Brush over cooled tart. Slice and serve.

Carrville Inn

The Carrville Inn was built in 1854 as a stop on the California-Oregon stage road during the California Gold Rush. Set on 25 acres at the north end of Trinity Lake, this beautifully restored, historic country inn offers superb accommodations, fine food and breathtaking scenery.

Sweeping lawns and flowerbeds can be enjoyed from both the upper and lower verandas. A variety of barnyard and exotic animals remind you that this is truly a country inn. A hearty country breakfast features eggs from the inn's hens and berries and fruit from the inn's garden.

INNKEEPERS:	Dave & Sheri Overly
ADDRESS:	3536 Carrville Loop Road
	Trinity Center, California 96091
TELEPHONE:	(530) 266-3511
E-MAIL:	info@carrvilleinn.com
WEBSITE:	www.carrvilleinn.com
ROOMS:	5 Rooms; Private & shared baths
CHILDREN:	Children age 10 and older welcome
ANIMALS:	Horse boarding available; Resident dog
HANDICAPPED:	Not handicapped accessible
DIETARY NEEDS:	Will accommodate guests' special dietary needs

Blackberry Cobbler

Makes 10 Servings

"This recipe came from our first guests. Our guests discover, while roaming the grounds, that our blackberries are plump and tasty. So they are surprised by a breakfast treat of blackberry cobbler that is not too sweet." ~ Innkeeper, Carrville Inn Bed & Breakfast

1½	cups sugar, divided
4	tablespoons plus 2 cups all-purpose flour, divided
8	cups fresh or frozen (thawed) blackberries, gently washed
5	tablespoons butter, cut into pieces
1	teaspoon salt
¾	cup shortening
5	tablespoons cold water, more or less

Whipped cream or ice cream, for serving

Preheat oven to 450°F. Spray bottom of a 9x13-inch baking pan with non-stick cooking spray. Sprinkle pan with ¾ cup of sugar. Sprinkle pan with 2 tablespoons of flour (use more or less flour, depending on how runny you like the fruit juices). Sprinkle with blackberries. Sprinkle with remaining ¾ cup of sugar. Sprinkle with 2 tablespoons of flour. Dot with butter.

In a large bowl, combine 2 cups of flour and salt. Cut in shortening with a pastry cutter or fork. Add enough water to make a dough. Form dough into a ball and roll out to fit pan. Lay dough on top of fruit. Trim dough to fit pan. Spear dough with a knife to make vents. Bake for 15 minutes. Lower oven temperature to 350°F and bake for 30 minutes longer. Serve with whipped cream or ice cream.

Note: This recipe was created for breakfast and is not too sweet. Add more sugar for a sweeter cobbler. Depending on the season, you can substitute sliced, peeled apricots or peaches for the blackberries.

Babbling Brook Inn

The Babbling Brook Inn

Cascading waterfalls, a meandering brook and a romantic garden gazebo grace an acre of gardens, pines and redwoods surrounding this secluded, urban inn. Built in 1909 on the foundation of an 1870s tannery, a 1790s grist mill and a 2,000-year-old Indian fishing village, the Babbling Brook Inn is the oldest and largest bed & breakfast in the Santa Cruz area.

Rooms are decorated in styles representing the works of Old World artists and poets such as Monet, Tennyson, Degas, Cezanne and Renoir. Each has a cozy featherbed and delightful views of the gardens and brook.

INNKEEPERS:	Aurorah Cheney
ADDRESS:	1025 Laural Street
	Santa Cruz, California 95060
TELEPHONE:	(831) 427-2437; (800) 866-1131
E-MAIL:	aurorah@innsbythesea.com
WEBSITE:	www.innsbythesea.com
ROOMS:	13 Rooms; Private baths
CHILDREN:	Welcome
ANIMALS:	Not allowed
HANDICAPPED:	Not handicapped accessible
DIETARY NEEDS:	Will accommodate guests' special dietary needs

Apple Cranberry Crisp

Makes 6 to 8 Servings

5	Granny Smith apples, peeled and sliced into wedges
½	cup cranberries (or raspberries or raisins)
¾	cup all-purpose flour
1	stick plus 2⅔ tablespoons butter
2	teaspoons cinnamon
¾	cup old-fashioned or quick-cooking oats
¼	teaspoon salt
1	cup granola
1	cup packed brown sugar

Ice cream or whipped cream, for serving (optional)

Preheat oven to 375°F. Fill a greased 8x8-inch baking pan with cranberries and apples. Put flour and butter in a bowl. Rub butter into flour with your hands until mixture resembles coarse crumbs. Add cinnamon, oats, salt, granola and brown sugar; combine well and sprinkle over fruit in pan.

Bake for 40 minutes, until top is browned and apples are tender (check after 30 minutes and cover with foil to prevent burning, if needed). Serve warm with ice cream or whipped cream, if desired.

The Grateful Bed

This prominent, circa 1905 Victorian home was lovingly restored in 1998. The innkeepers, purveyors of nostalgic comfort, have furnished the inn with lovely antiques, quality beds and timeless treasures. The inn, located in the tree-lined Avenues of Chico, offers richly appointed bed chambers with fine linens and luxurious baths.

The inn is just a stone's throw from California State University, Bidwell Mansion State Historic Park and downtown Chico's numerous shops and restaurants.

INNKEEPERS:	Rick & Carol Turner
ADDRESS:	1462 Arcadian Avenue
	Chico, California 95926
TELEPHONE:	(530) 342-2464
E-MAIL:	thegratefulbed@chico.com
WEBSITE:	www.chico.com/grateful
ROOMS:	4 Rooms; Private baths
CHILDREN:	Children age 12 and older welcome
ANIMALS:	Not allowed; Resident dogs
HANDICAPPED:	Not handicapped accessible
DIETARY NEEDS:	Call ahead

Ginger Snap Peach Crisp

Makes 6 Servings

6	cups sliced fresh or frozen peeled peaches
¾	cup packed brown sugar
¼	cup all-purpose flour
½	cup quick-cooking oats
5⅓	tablespoons butter, softened or melted
6	ginger snap cookies, crushed

Amaretto, to taste

4	mint sprigs, for garnish

Preheat oven to 375°F. Lightly spray 6 (4-ounce) ramekins with non-stick cooking spray. Fill ramekins with peach slices (slightly overfill, as peaches will cook down). Combine brown sugar, flour, oats, butter and crushed ginger snaps; sprinkle over peaches in each ramekin. Drizzle with Amaretto. Place ramekins on a cookie sheet and bake for about 35 minutes, until bubbling. Garnish with mint sprigs to serve.

Barney's Rancho Bernardo

B arney's Rancho Bernardo Bed & Breakfast is a 40-acre cattle ranch located in secluded Cathey's Valley. Expansive vistas of rolling hills dotted with ancient oak trees, Chinese rock walls, springs and grazing livestock surround the ranch and guest houses, making Rancho Bernardo more like a resort than a bed & breakfast.

Rancho Bernardo is ideally located near Yosemite National Park, the ghost town of Hornitos, Lakes Bagby and McClure, gold panning, skiing, river rafting on the mighty Merced River and a host of other activities.

INNKEEPERS:	Kathleen and Barney Lozares
ADDRESS:	2617 Old Highway South
	Cathey's Valley, California 95306
TELEPHONE:	(209) 966-4511; (877) 930-1669
E-MAIL:	kathleen@ranchobernardobnb.com
WEBSITE:	www.ranchobernardobnb.com
ROOMS:	1 Suite; 1 Guest House; Private baths
CHILDREN:	Children age 8 and older welcome
ANIMALS:	Not allowed; Resident horses, cattle & cat
HANDICAPPED:	Not handicapped accessible
DIETARY NEEDS:	Will accommodate guests' special dietary needs

Boysenberry Cobbler

Makes 6 Servings

"This cobbler can be made with any berry. It's great at breakfast or served with ice cream for dessert – everyone loves it." ~ Innkeeper, Barney's Rancho Bernardo Bed & Breakfast

1	stick butter
1	cup all-purpose flour
1	cup plus 2 tablespoons sugar
2	tablespoons baking powder
1	teaspoon salt
1	cup milk
4	cups boysenberries (or other berries)

Preheat oven to 350°F. Spray a 7x11-inch or 8x8-inch baking dish with non-stick cooking spray. Put butter in baking dish. Put baking dish in oven until butter melts. Combine flour, 1 cup of sugar, baking powder and salt. Add milk and stir to combine. Press flour mixture into baking dish. Spread berries and any berry juice over flour mixture. Sprinkle 2 tablespoons of sugar over berries. Bake for 30-35 minutes. Serve and enjoy.

McCaffrey House Inn

The McCaffrey House Bed & Breakfast Inn is an AAA Four-Diamond inn nestled in a quiet forest hollow in the California mountains, where majestic oak, cedar and pine trees mark the edge of the Stanislaus National Forest and Emigrant Wilderness. A delightfully warm and charming country home in the California Gold Country, the inn was designed and built by innkeepers Michael and Stephanie McCaffrey.

Each morning, a full breakfast is served in the dining room. A delightful picnic lunch is available for guests with a taste for the simple pleasures in life.

INNKEEPERS:	Michael & Stephanie McCaffrey
ADDRESS:	23251 Highway 108
	Twain Harte, California 95383
TELEPHONE:	(209) 586-0757; (888) 586-0757
E-MAIL:	innkeeper@mccaffreyhouse.com
WEBSITE:	www.mccaffreyhouse.com
ROOMS:	7 Rooms; 1 Suite; Private baths
CHILDREN:	Children age 6 months and older welcome
ANIMALS:	Not allowed; Resident cat & dogs
HANDICAPPED:	Handicapped accessible
DIETARY NEEDS:	Will accommodate guests' special dietary needs

Baked Bananas

Makes 6 Servings

"We serve this on cold winter mornings. An entrée follows." ~ Innkeeper,
McCaffrey House Bed & Breakfast Inn

6	ripe, but firm bananas, sliced
1½	cups orange juice
1	teaspoon vanilla extract
½	cup all-purpose flour
½	cup quick-cooking oats
¾	cup packed brown sugar
½	teaspoon nutmeg
½	teaspoon salt
¾	stick butter, chilled

Whipped cream or ice cream, for serving

Preheat oven to 375°F. Divide banana slices among 6 greased 1-cup ramekins or custard cups. Combine orange juice and vanilla; pour over bananas. Combine flour, oats, brown sugar, nutmeg and salt. Cut in butter until mixture resembles small peas; spoon evenly over bananas. Bake for 15-20 minutes. Serve warm with whipped cream or ice cream.

Martine Inn

R anked as one of the "Top Eight B&Bs in Historic Homes" by *Bon Appétit*, the Martine Inn is an elegant getaway for the discerning traveler. With soft robes, fresh fruit in silver baskets, an acclaimed restaurant with an extensive wine and champagne list and delightful rose gardens across the grounds, guests are sure to enjoy a luxurious stay.

From the dining room, look directly out at the waves crashing against the rocky coastline of Pacific Grove on Monterey Bay. On clear days, Mt. Madonna is visible 50 miles across the bay.

INNKEEPERS:	Don Martine
ADDRESS:	255 Ocean View Boulevard
	Pacific Grove, California 93950
TELEPHONE:	(831) 373-3388; (800) 852-5588
E-MAIL:	don@martineinn.com
WEBSITE:	www.martineinn.com
ROOMS:	24 Rooms; Private baths
CHILDREN:	Not encouraged
ANIMALS:	Not allowed
HANDICAPPED:	Handicapped accessible
DIETARY NEEDS:	Will accommodate guests' special dietary needs

Baked Pears with Caramel Sauce

Makes 6 Servings

3   pears, stemmed, halved and cored
6   tablespoons butter, divided
6   tablespoons brown sugar, divided
Nutmeg
¼   cup brandy
¼   cup water
½   cup heavy cream
Fresh mint sprigs, for garnish
Ice cream, for serving (optional)

Preheat oven to 375°F. Place pears, cut-side-up, in a baking dish. Place 1 tablespoon of butter and 1 tablespoon of brown sugar in core of each pear half. Sprinkle lightly with nutmeg. Sprinkle with brandy. Pour water into pan. Cover with foil and bake for 45 minutes, until pears are tender.

Place 1 pear half, cut-side-down, on each plate. Pour juices from baking dish into a saucepan over medium heat. Scrape "caramel" from bottom of baking dish into saucepan. Add heavy cream and cook, stirring constantly, until sauce is thickened and a caramel color. Drizzle cream mixture over pears. Place a sprig of fresh mint at end of each pear half to resemble pear stem and leaves. Serve warm with ice cream, if desired.

Avalon

Imagine an enchanted forest. In a clearing, a Tudor home is nestled amidst towering redwoods. On the expansive deck, afternoon tea and cookies await. In the sunny meadow, comfortable chairs beckon. The unique decor and original hand-painted murals let you to step into another world.

The exquisite suites are the ultimate place for a fantasy getaway. Amenities include king-size beds, luxury linens, down comforters and pillows, private entrances, fireplaces and large baths with steam showers and hot tubs.

INNKEEPERS:	Hillary & Gary McCalla
ADDRESS:	11910 Graton Road
	Sebastopol, California 95472
TELEPHONE:	(707) 824-0880; (877) 328-2566
E-MAIL:	info@avalonluxuryinn.com
WEBSITE:	www.avalonluxuryinn.com
ROOMS:	3 Suites; Private baths
CHILDREN:	Call ahead
ANIMALS:	Not allowed; Resident cat
HANDICAPPED:	Not handicapped accessible
DIETARY NEEDS:	Will accommodate guests' special dietary needs

Butter Rum Apples

Makes 6 Servings

6	Gravenstein or Granny Smith apples, peeled and quartered
1	cup dark rum
1	cup sugar
1	teaspoon cinnamon
½	teaspoon nutmeg
½	stick butter

Whipped cream and/or vanilla ice cream, for serving

Preheat oven to 350°F. Place apples, rum, sugar, cinnamon, nutmeg and butter in a large saucepan. Add enough water to cover apples. Bring to a boil, lower heat and simmer until apples are tender. Serve 4 apple quarters per person. If desired, reduce pan juices to a syrup consistency and drizzle over each serving. Serve with whipped cream and/or ice cream.

Carriage House

Come experience the beauty of the Point Reyes National Seashore, a coastal wilderness abundant with wildlife and just one hour north of San Francisco. The Carriage House Bed & Breakfast is located just outside the village of Point Reyes Station, adjacent to the Point Reyes National Seashore. Days spent in nature are enhanced by the gracious, comfortable suites and beautiful garden.

Enjoy 150 miles of hiking, biking and horseback riding trails and numerous, pristine ocean and bay beaches perfect for long walks and relaxation.

INNKEEPERS:	Felicity Kirsch
ADDRESS:	325 Mesa Road
	Point Reyes, California 94956
TELEPHONE:	(415) 663-8627; (800) 613-8351
E-MAIL:	felicity@carriagehousebb.com
WEBSITE:	www.carriagehousebb.com
ROOMS:	1 Room; 3 Suites; Private baths
CHILDREN:	Welcome
ANIMALS:	Not allowed
HANDICAPPED:	Not handicapped accessible
DIETARY NEEDS:	Will accommodate guests' special dietary needs

Pears with Goat Cheese & Fig Preserves

Makes 8 Servings

4	medium Comice pears (or other seasonal pears), peeled, halved lengthwise and cored
¼	cup lemon juice
4	ounces goat cheese, crumbled
½	cup fig preserves

Toss pear halves with lemon juice. Thinly slice pear halves, cutting to, but not through, stem ends. Fan a pear half on each plate. Sprinkle with 2 tablespoons of goat cheese and top with 1 tablespoon of fig preserves.

Coxhead House Inn

Steven G. Cabrera

Hidden quietly in the San Francisco peninsula's reflective past, you'll find this historic, 1891 Tudor Revival bed & breakfast that offers the rustic pleasures of days gone by. A bit of England comes alive in a leisurely atmosphere with gardens and comfortably elegant accommodations.

The home was built as a country retreat by Ernest A. Coxhead, a noted English architect. Coxhead used the English rural vernacular, with a double bowed roof and delicate, leaded glass windows to add charm to his English cottage. The home has survived, almost untouched, for over a century.

INNKEEPERS:	Steve Cabrera & Pat Osborn
ADDRESS:	37 East Santa Inez Avenue
	San Mateo, California 94401
TELEPHONE:	(650) 685-1600
E-MAIL:	coxhead@coxhead.com
WEBSITE:	www.coxhead.com
ROOMS:	5 Rooms; Private & shared baths
CHILDREN:	Welcome
ANIMALS:	Not allowed
HANDICAPPED:	Not handicapped accessible
DIETARY NEEDS:	Will accommodate guests' special dietary needs

Banana Fritters

Makes 4 to 5 Servings

"This was my grandmother's recipe. She sometimes substituted four, thinly sliced, tart green apples for the bananas." ~ Innkeeper, Coxhead House Bed & Breakfast Inn

1	egg
½	cup milk
1	cup all-purpose flour, divided
1½	tablespoons lemon juice
1	teaspoon baking powder
3-4	tablespoons vegetable oil
4	very ripe bananas
3	tablespoons powdered sugar

In a bowl, beat egg and milk with a mixer. Gradually beat in ½ cup of flour. Beat in lemon juice. Add remaining ½ cup of flour and baking powder; beat just until blended.

Heat oil in skillet over medium heat. Slice each banana crosswise into 3 equal pieces. Slice each piece in half lengthwise. With a fork, dip 3 banana slices at a time into egg mixture, coating thoroughly.

Gently transfer each banana piece to skillet. Cook just until golden brown on each side. Remove cooked banana slices to paper towels to drain, then quickly transfer to a warm plate. Arrange 5-6 banana slices in a flower pattern on each plate. Dust entire plate with powdered sugar and serve.

Whispering Pines

On January 24, 1848, gold was discovered in the Coloma Valley. Columbia, south of this site, was one of hundreds of settlements that sprang up in the wake of the Gold Rush. Whispering Pines Bed & Breakfast is located in the beautiful whispering pines of Gold Country in the Sierra Nevada foothills. The inn is just one mile from Columbia and Railtown 1897 State Historic Parks and close to Yosemite National Park.

The Great Room feature a large brick fireplace where you can read or visit with your fellow guests. Or, relax on the back porch in the afternoon sun.

INNKEEPERS:	Earl & Sylvia Brewer
ADDRESS:	22055 Parrotts Ferry Road
	Sonora, California 95370
TELEPHONE:	(800) 649-0152
E-MAIL:	innkeepers@whispering-pines-bnb.com
WEBSITE:	www.whispering-pines-bnb.com
ROOMS:	3 Rooms; Private baths
CHILDREN:	Welcome
ANIMALS:	Not allowed; Resident dog
HANDICAPPED:	Not handicapped accessible
DIETARY NEEDS:	Will accommodate guests' special dietary needs

Hot Curried Fruit

Makes 10 to 12 Servings

"This recipe is easy and always receives compliments." ~ Innkeeper, Whispering Pines Bed & Breakfast

1	(29-ounce) can apricot halves, drained
1	(29-ounce) can pear halves, drained
1	(29-ounce) can peach halves, drained
1	(20-ounce) can pineapple chunks, drained
¾	cup golden raisins
½	stick butter or margarine
½	cup packed brown sugar
1	teaspoon curry powder, or more to taste

Preheat oven to 400°F. Combine fruit and raisins in a 2½-quart casserole dish. Melt butter in a small saucepan over low heat. Add brown sugar and curry powder; cook, stirring, until brown sugar is dissolved. Pour butter mixture over fruit. Cover and bake for 30 minutes, or until heated through.

Melitta Station Inn

The Melitta Station Inn is one of Sonoma County's most romantic bed & breakfast inns. The innkeepers bring their unique brand of English hospitality to this historic property. Conveniently located in the middle of the Northern California Wine Country, Melitta Station has something to offer everyone.

A full, elegant country breakfast is served in the great room or on the deck where you can watch hummingbirds and finches feed. Tasty delights include Jackie's fruit appetizers, stratas, frittatas, quiches and omelets.

INNKEEPERS:	Jackie & Tim Thresh
ADDRESS:	5850 Melitta Road
	Santa Rosa, California 95409
TELEPHONE:	(707) 538-7712; (800) 504-3099
E-MAIL:	info@melittastationinn.com
WEBSITE:	www.melittastationinn.com
ROOMS:	5 Rooms; 1 Suite; Private baths
CHILDREN:	Welcome
ANIMALS:	Not allowed; Resident dog
HANDICAPPED:	Not handicapped accessible
DIETARY NEEDS:	Will accommodate guests' special dietary needs

Raspberry Terrine

Makes 6 to 8 Servings

"This is a unique way to serve fruit for breakfast. The raspberry and biscuit combination is reminiscent of 'crowdie,' a traditional Scottish dessert. Plan ahead – the terrine needs to freeze overnight." ~ Innkeeper, Melitta Station Inn

2	large egg whites
⅓	cup powdered sugar, sifted
8	ounces mascarpone cheese
1	cup plain whole milk yogurt
½	pound raspberries (or sliced strawberries, peaches, etc.)
½	pound Amaretti cookies, broken into pieces*

Sorbet, for serving
Orange slices, for garnish
Mint leaves, for garnish

Line a 9x5-inch loaf pan with parchment paper. Beat egg whites until stiff. Gradually whisk in powdered sugar. Gently fold in mascarpone cheese and yogurt. Stir in raspberries and cookie pieces. Pour mixture into loaf, cover and freeze overnight.

Just before serving, put terrine in refrigerator for 10 minutes, then turn terrine out of pan. Slice and serve with sorbet. Garnish with orange slices and mint leaves.

*Note: Amaretti cookies are crunchy Italian almond cookies, often found in a distinctive red tin from the company, Lazzaroni. They are available at Italian and specialty food stores and Trader Joe's.

Sterling Gardens

Sterling Gardens Bed & Breakfast is located on Kincaid Flat, the site of the former Kincaid Gold Mine. Oaks and other trees provide a habitat for numerous birds of an ever-changing seasonal variety and the beautiful Country English home and variegated flower gardens compliment a vista of a pond and wooded hills.

A gourmet breakfast is served in the elegant, oak-paneled dining room. Enjoy the tree-shaded garden or relax in the spacious, comfortable living room with a fireplace, game table and wine and refreshment bar.

INNKEEPERS:	Carl & Charlotte Tucker
ADDRESS:	18047 Lime Kiln Road
	Sonora, California 95370
TELEPHONE:	(209) 533-9300; (888) 533-9301
E-MAIL:	ctucker@mlode.com
WEBSITE:	www.sterlinggardens.com
ROOMS:	4 Rooms; Private baths
CHILDREN:	Children age 12 and older welcome
ANIMALS:	Not allowed
HANDICAPPED:	Not handicapped accessible
DIETARY NEEDS:	Will accommodate guests' special dietary needs

Pickled Cherries

Makes 10 to 12 Pints

"These are great to make in the heart of the summer and then serve with your turkey on Thanksgiving. They also make great Christmas gifts for friends and family." - Innkeeper, Sterling Gardens Bed & Breakfast

4¼   cups white wine vinegar
1   pound soft light brown sugar or white sugar
6   whole cloves
6   juniper berries, lightly crushed
Thinly sliced peel of 1 lemon
1   (2-inch) cinnamon stick
2   pounds Morello, Kentish Red or Montmorency cherries

Combine all ingredients, except cherries, in a stainless steel or enameled saucepan. Bring to a boil, lower heat and simmer for 10 minutes. Cover and let stand overnight to infuse vinegar.

Pick over cherries and cut stems down to 1-inch-long (discard any damaged ones). Rinse and dry cherries thoroughly, then pack them into small preserving jars (jam jars can be used if they have close-fitting plastic lids – metal screw-top lids react badly to contact with vinegar).*

Strain vinegar mixture over cherries, completely covering cherries. Seal jars and store in a dark, dry place for at least 1 month before using.

*Note: Follow canning safety practices and sterilize all equipment.

Alegria Oceanfront Inn

A legria Oceanfront Inn is located on a bluff overlooking Big River Beach and an ever changing ocean cove. Nestled in historic Main Street in Mendocino Village, the inn is just steps away from unique shops, beautiful galleries and fine dining. Six state parks and reserves are within 15 minutes, offering unlimited hiking, biking and breathtaking views.

To celebrate Northern California's renowned cuisine, the inn offers cooking classes, demonstrations and book signings with celebrity chefs.

INNKEEPERS:	Eric & Elaine Hillesland
ADDRESS:	44781 Main Street
	Mendocino, California 95460
TELEPHONE:	(707) 937-5150; (800) 780-7905
E-MAIL:	inn@oceanfrontmagic.com
WEBSITE:	www.oceanfrontmagic.com
ROOMS:	7 Rooms; Private baths
CHILDREN:	Welcome; Call ahead
ANIMALS:	Not allowed
HANDICAPPED:	Not handicapped accessible
DIETARY NEEDS:	Will accommodate guests' special dietary needs

More Than Chocolate Chip Cookies

Makes About 60 Cookies

2	sticks unsalted butter, softened
¾	cup white sugar
1	cup packed brown sugar
2	large eggs
1½	teaspoons vanilla extract
2½	cups all-purpose flour
1	teaspoon baking soda
1	teaspoon cinnamon
½	teaspoon salt
½	cup chopped dried apricots
1	cup old-fashioned rolled oats
½	cup cacao nibs (by Scharffen Berger)*
2	cups semi-sweet chocolate chips
½	cup dried cranberries

Preheat oven to 375°F. In a large bowl, cream together butter and white and brown sugar. Add eggs and vanilla; mix well. In a small bowl, combine flour, baking soda, cinnamon and salt; add to butter mixture and mix thoroughly. Fold in dried apricots, oats, cacao nibs, chocolate chips and dried cranberries. Drop dough by teaspoonsful onto a non-stick or greased cookie sheet. Bake for 8-10 minutes. Cool cookies on wire racks.

*Note: Scharffen Berger cacao nibs are roasted cocoa beans separated from their husks and broken into small bits. The essence of chocolate, the nibs add crunchiness and subtle chocolate flavor to baked goods and savory dishes. They make a great substitute for nuts or chocolate chips, without added sweetness. Cacao nibs are available at gourmet stores and some natural food stores.

Captain's Inn at Moss Landing

Enjoy wonderful waterfront views from the Captain's Inn at Moss Landing. View all sorts of wildlife including birds and harbor seals. Sit next to the river as it heads out to the sea or gaze at distant Fremont's Peak. The inn is located in the middle of beautiful Monterey Bay, near Monterey and Santa Cruz. It is just a short walk to sandy beaches, the ocean, harbor, dining, art galleries and antique shopping,

Rooms include soaking tubs, fireplaces and fresh flowers. Breakfasts feature traditional recipes from German grandmothers.

INNKEEPERS:	Captain Yohn & Melanie Gideon
ADDRESS:	8122 Moss Landing Road
	Moss Landing, California 95039
TELEPHONE:	(831) 633-5550
E-MAIL:	res@captainsinn.com
WEBSITE:	www.captainsinn.com
ROOMS:	10 Rooms; Private baths
CHILDREN:	Children age 12 and older welcome
ANIMALS:	Not allowed; Resident dog
HANDICAPPED:	Handicapped accessible
DIETARY NEEDS:	Will accommodate guests' special dietary needs

Double Chocolate
Oatmeal Cookies

Makes 24 Cookies

"Be sure to have plenty of cold milk on hand when serving. Oatmeal and chocolate are both good for you!" - Innkeeper, Captain's Inn at Moss Landing

1½	cups sugar
2	sticks butter, softened
1	egg
½	cup water
1	teaspoon vanilla extract
1½	cups all-purpose flour
⅓	cup unsweetened cocoa powder
½	teaspoon baking soda
½	teaspoon salt
3	cups old-fashioned rolled oats
6	ounces semi-sweet chocolate chips
¼	cup chopped pecans

In a large bowl, cream together sugar and butter. Beat in egg, water and vanilla. In a medium bowl, combine flour, cocoa, baking soda and salt; add to butter mixture and mix until well blended. Stir in oats, chocolate chips and pecans. Cover and chill dough for 1 hour.

Preheat oven to 350°F. Roll dough into balls, using about 2 tablespoons of dough per ball. Bake on a non-stick cookie sheet for 10-12 minutes.

The Napa Inn

The Napa Inn, a beautiful circa 1899, Queen Anne Victorian furnished with antiques reminiscent of a bygone era, was built as a wedding gift. Today, the inn retains the charm and romantic aura of its origins. Located on a quiet street in historic downtown Napa, the inn is within an easy stroll of shops and restaurants. Golf, hot air ballooning, horseback riding and the Napa Valley Wine Train are just some of the attractions awaiting you.

Relax in the quiet gardens with an afternoon refreshment, or relish a cup of the inn's specially blended coffee in front of a cozy fire in the parlor.

INNKEEPERS:	Brooke & Jim Boyer
ADDRESS:	1137 Warren Street
	Napa, California 94559
TELEPHONE:	(707) 257-1444; (800) 435-1144
E-MAIL:	info@napainn.com
WEBSITE:	www.napainn.com
ROOMS:	9 Rooms; 4 Suites; 1 Cottage; Private baths
CHILDREN:	Welcome
ANIMALS:	Dogs welcome; Resident outdoor cats
HANDICAPPED:	Handicapped accessible
DIETARY NEEDS:	Will accommodate guests' special dietary needs

Apricot Shortbread

Makes 8 Servings

1½   cups coarsely chopped dried apricots
1   stick butter, softened
1⅓   cups all-purpose flour, divided
⅓   cup plus ⅔-¾ cup sugar
¼   cup water
1   large egg, beaten
¼   teaspoon salt
½   teaspoon baking powder
Powdered sugar, for garnish

Soak apricots overnight in hot water to cover. The next day, preheat oven to 375°F. Combine butter, 1 cup of flour and ⅓ cup of sugar; mix with a spoon or your hands until smooth. Pat dough over bottom of a 9-inch pie pan. Bake for about 25 minutes, or until golden brown.

Drain apricots. Combine apricots and water in a skillet over high heat. When mixture begins to bubble, lower heat to medium. Cook, stirring often (so fruit doesn't scorch), until mixture thickens. Remove from heat and cool. When cool, add egg to apricot mixture and mix well.

In a bowl, combine ⅔-¾ cup of sugar (depending on sweetness of apricots) with remaining ⅓ cup of flour, salt and baking powder; beat until smooth. Spread apricot mixture over crust and bake for 25 minutes, or until puffy. Remove from oven and cool slightly. Dust with powdered sugar. Cut into wedges and serve.

Camellia Inn

The Camellia Inn, a charming 1869 Italianate Victorian inn, is located in the heart of the Sonoma County Wine Country. More than 50 varieties of camellias bloom on the inn's landscaped grounds, surrounding the villa-style swimming pool. Interior architectural treasures include twin marble fireplaces, beautiful double parlors and inlaid hardwood floors.

Don't miss "Chocolate Covered Wednesdays," a day of chocolate decadence from morning chocolate croissants to evening chocolate truffles and port.

INNKEEPERS:	Del Lewand
ADDRESS:	211 North Street
	Healdsburg, California 95448
TELEPHONE:	(707) 433-8182; (800) 727-8182
E-MAIL:	lucy@camelliainn.com
WEBSITE:	www.camelliainn.com
ROOMS:	9 Rooms; Private baths
CHILDREN:	Welcome
ANIMALS:	Not allowed
HANDICAPPED:	Not handicapped accessible
DIETARY NEEDS:	Will accommodate guests' special dietary needs

Cappuccino Thins

Makes About 60 Cookies

4	ounces sweet baking chocolate, coarsely chopped
½	cup plus 2 tablespoons white sugar
½	cup packed brown sugar
1	egg yolk
1	tablespoon instant coffee powder
1	tablespoon unsweetened cocoa powder
1	teaspoon cinnamon
¾	teaspoon salt
2	sticks unsalted butter, cut into pieces and softened
1	cup cake flour
1	cup unbleached all-purpose flour

Chop chocolate in a food processor until it resembles small crumbs; transfer to a small bowl and set aside. In a medium bowl, combine white and brown sugar, egg yolk, coffee powder, cocoa, cinnamon and salt; mix for 1 minute, then transfer to food processor. Add butter; process for 1 minute. Add cake and all-purpose flour and chopped chocolate; pulse just until flour is incorporated (do not overmix).

Divide dough into 4 pieces. Shape into 1-inch thick, round logs, wrap in plastic wrap and chill for 1 hour (can be frozen). Preheat oven to 350°F. Cut dough into ¼-inch-thick slices and bake for 8 minutes.

Lakeport English Inn

The Lakeport English Inn is comprised of a pair of historic Victorian homes wrapped around a stunning English garden. Lively rooms burst with elegance and tradition. This "glimpse of England" boasts a billiard room, whirlpool tubs and a pub. Indulge in high tea on weekend afternoons, complete with scones, Devonshire cream and strawberry jam.

You will be greeted with a tray of goodies, just as if you were arriving at your own English country house. In the evening, you will receive turndown service, which includes a very British bedtime treat.

INNKEEPERS:	Karan & Hugh Mackey
ADDRESS:	675 North Main Street
	Lakeport, California 95453
TELEPHONE:	(707) 263-4317
E-MAIL:	lakeportenglishinn@mchsi.com
WEBSITE:	www.lakeportenglishinn.com
ROOMS:	5 Rooms; Private baths
CHILDREN:	Welcome
ANIMALS:	Not allowed
HANDICAPPED:	Not handicapped accessible
DIETARY NEEDS:	Will accommodate guests' special dietary needs

Dingle Dangle Gingerbread Squares

Makes About 30

"These cookies are so addicting that it is essential to make only one batch." ~
Innkeeper, Lakeport English Inn

½	stick butter, melted
1	cup packed brown sugar
1	large egg
1	teaspoon vanilla extract
½	cup all-purpose flour
2	tablespoons old-fashioned rolled oats
½	teaspoon salt
1	teaspoon baking powder
1	cup coarsely chopped walnuts
½	cup chopped candied ginger

Preheat oven to 350°F. In a large bowl, combine butter and brown sugar. Mix in egg and vanilla. In a medium bowl, combine flour, oats, salt and baking powder; stir into butter mixture. Stir in walnuts and candied ginger.

Pour batter into a non-stick or greased 8x8-inch baking pan. Bake for 25-30 minutes (do not overbake – gingerbread should be dry on the outside and firm in the center). Cool gingerbread in pan, then cut into squares.

Prufrock's Garden Inn

Experience the magic of Prufrock's Garden Inn, a special place tucked between the ocean and magnificent mountain wilderness in a community known for its orchards and flower fields. The surrounding beach-front town is friendly and unpretentious. For those who want a big-city feel, Santa Barbara is only ten minutes away.

The Afternoon Delight is a gardenside, two-room suite with Jacuzzi tub, two patios and Dutch doors. It is the ultimate luxury experience and is perfect for those seeking romance.

INNKEEPERS:	Judy & Jim Halvorsen
ADDRESS:	600 Linden Avenue
	Carpinteria, California 93013
TELEPHONE:	(805) 566-9696; (877) 837-6257
E-MAIL:	innkeepers@prufrocks.com
WEBSITE:	www.prufrocks.com
ROOMS:	7 Rooms; 2 Suites; 2 Cottages; Private baths
CHILDREN:	Children welcome
ANIMALS:	Not allowed; Resident cat
HANDICAPPED:	Handicapped accessible
DIETARY NEEDS:	Will accommodate guests' special dietary needs

Crunchy-Chewy Ginger Snaps

Makes 48 Cookies

"Guests can't leave these ginger snaps alone. The combination of a crunchy crust and chewy center make them an inn favorite. The recipe came from Grandma Halvorsen." ~ Innkeeper, Prufrock's Garden Inn

¾	cup shortening
1	cup packed brown sugar
¼	cup molasses
1	large egg
2¼	cups all-purpose flour, sifted
2	teaspoons baking soda
½	teaspoon salt
1	teaspoon ground ginger
1	teaspoon cinnamon
½	teaspoon ground cloves

White sugar

Preheat oven to 375°F. In a large bowl, cream together shortening, brown sugar, molasses and egg until fluffy. In a medium bowl, combine flour, baking soda, salt, ginger, cinnamon and cloves. Slowly add flour mixture to molasses mixture, stirring to combine.

Form dough into balls slightly smaller than golf balls. Roll balls in white sugar. Place balls 2-inches apart on a greased cookie sheet. Bake for about 10 minutes, or until cracks show on cookies. Cool briefly, then remove from cookie sheet.

Victorian Garden Inn

The Victorian Garden Inn is a historic, circa 1870 farmhouse named for the lush English gardens surrounding it. Just a short walk from Sonoma's historic town plaza in Northern California's famed Wine Country, the inn offers guests an exceptional lodging experience.

A gourmet breakfast features healthful Sonoma County products. Enjoy a tantalizing assortment of fresh fruit, scrumptious pastries and muffins, granola and local cheeses served in the dining room, the gardens or on a wicker tray delivered to your door.

INNKEEPERS:	Donna Lewis
ADDRESS:	316 East Napa Street
	Sonoma, California 95476
TELEPHONE:	(707) 996-5339; (800) 543-5339
E-MAIL:	vgardeninn@aol.com
WEBSITE:	www.victoriangardeninn.com
ROOMS:	2 Rooms; 1 Suite; 1 Cottage; Private & shared baths
CHILDREN:	Children age 12 and older welcome
ANIMALS:	Not allowed; Resident outdoor cat
HANDICAPPED:	Not handicapped accessible
DIETARY NEEDS:	Will accommodate guests' special dietary needs

Aunt Alice's Persimmon Cookies

Makes 24 Cookies

"I make these moist, chewy cookies with organic persimmons." ~ Innkeeper, Victorian Garden Inn

2	cups all-purpose flour
1	teaspoon baking soda
1	teaspoon cinnamon
½	teaspoon nutmeg
½	teaspoon ground cloves
1	cup white sugar
1	cup packed brown sugar
1	cup shortening
1	egg
1	cup persimmon pulp*
1	cup chopped walnuts
1	cup raisins

Preheat oven to 350°F. In a large bowl, mix flour, baking soda, cinnamon, nutmeg and cloves. In a medium bowl, mix white and brown sugar and shortening until smooth. Mix in egg. Stir in persimmon. Add persimmon mixture to flour mixture; stir to combine well. Stir in walnuts and raisins. Drop dough by teaspoonsful onto a greased cookie sheet. Bake for about 12-15 minutes, until golden brown.

*Note: Persimmons are available from October to February.

Stahlecker House

Secluded on one and a half acres of lush, manicured lawns and flowering gardens, the Stahlecker House Bed & Breakfast is a nostalgic gem in Napa Valley. Built in the late 1940s on the grounds of an apple orchard, the property now houses the beautifully decorated inn of vintage race car driver and pilot Ron and local artist and wife Ethel Stahlecker.

Sip fresh made lemonade on the sun deck or unwind in front of two fireplaces in the gathering rooms on a cool night. There are fireplaces in each bedroom and homemade cookies to satisfy any guest's sweet tooth.

INNKEEPERS:	Ron & Ethel Stahlecker
ADDRESS:	1042 Easum Drive
	Napa, California 94558
TELEPHONE:	(707) 257-1588; (800) 799-1588
E-MAIL:	stahlbnb@aol.com
WEBSITE:	www.stahleckerhouse.com
ROOMS:	4 Rooms; 1 Suite; Private baths
CHILDREN:	Welcome
ANIMALS:	Not allowed
HANDICAPPED:	Not handicapped accessible
DIETARY NEEDS:	Will accommodate guests' special dietary needs

Deluxe Chocolate Marshmallow Bars

Makes About 36 Bars

1½	sticks butter
1½	cups sugar
3	eggs
1	teaspoon vanilla extract
1⅓	cups all-purpose flour
½	teaspoon baking powder
½	teaspoon salt
3	tablespoons unsweetened cocoa powder
½	cup chopped nuts (optional)
4	cups miniature marshmallows

Topping:

1⅓	cups chocolate chips
3	tablespoons butter or margarine
1	cup peanut butter
2	cups crisp rice cereal

Preheat oven to 350°F. In a large bowl, cream together butter and sugar. Add eggs and vanilla; beat until fluffy. In a small bowl, combine flour, baking powder, salt and cocoa powder; add to butter mixture and mix well. Stir in nuts, if desired. Spread batter in a greased jelly roll pan.

Bake for 15-18 minutes. Remove from oven. Sprinkle with marshmallows. Return to oven and bake for 2-3 minutes longer. Using a knife dipped in water, spread marshmallows over cake. Cool, then spread topping over cake. Chill, then cut into bars.

For the topping: Combine chocolate chips, butter and peanut butter in a small saucepan over low heat. Cook, stirring constantly, until melted and combined. Remove from heat and gently stir in cereal.

Old Yacht Club Inn

Santa Barbara's beautiful East Beach is one block from the Old Yacht Club Inn. East Beach was rated one of the world's ten best beaches by the *L.A. Times*. Beach chairs, towels and bikes are provided by the inn.

Saturday dinner has been an Old Yacht Club tradition since 1980. Guests gather for champagne and are then seated for a five-course, prix fixe menu. The entrée typically incorporates the freshest and best fish available that day. Recipes such as artichokes Athena, salmon with raspberry beurre blanc sauce and chocolate cheesecake showcase the chef's talents.

INNKEEPERS:	Eilene Bruce
ADDRESS:	431 Corona Del Mar Drive
	Santa Barbara, California 93103
TELEPHONE:	(805) 962-1277; (800) 549-1676
E-MAIL:	info@oldyachtclubinn.com
WEBSITE:	www.oldyachtclubinn.com
ROOMS:	14 Rooms; 1 Suite; 1 Cottage; Private baths
CHILDREN:	Children age 12 and older welcome
ANIMALS:	Not allowed
HANDICAPPED:	Not handicapped accessible
DIETARY NEEDS:	Will accommodate guests' special dietary needs

Chocolate Cheesecake

Makes 16 Servings

Crust:

1	cup finely chopped almonds
2	tablespoons sugar
3	tablespoons butter, melted

Filling:

5	ounces semi-sweet chocolate
5	ounces milk chocolate
2	tablespoons butter
1/3	cup plus 2 tablespoons Amaretto
2	(8-ounce) packages cream cheese, cut into 8 pieces
2	large eggs
1/3	cup sugar
1	cup sour cream
1/2	cup whipping cream
1	(12-ounce) package frozen raspberries, thawed

For the crust: Preheat oven to 350°F. Put almonds in a 9-inch springform pan. Sprinkle sugar over nuts. Pour in melted butter. Mix with a fork and press into bottom of pan. Bake for 15-20 minutes, until lightly browned.

For the filling: Lower oven temperature to 325°F. Melt butter, semi-sweet and milk chocolate and 1/3 cup of Amaretto in a double boiler; whisk to combine. Put cream cheese in a food processor; pulse until softened. Add eggs; process to mix. Add sugar; process for 5-10 seconds. Scrape down sides of bowl. Add sour cream; process slightly.

With processor running, pour chocolate mixture into feed tube and process for 10-15 seconds. Scrape sides and bottom of processor bowl. Process for 5 seconds more. Pour filling into crust. Bake for 45 minutes. Turn oven off and prop door open 3-4 inches. Leave cheesecake in oven for 2 hours. Remove and cool to room temperature. (Refrigerate for up to 1 week.)

Whip cream until stiff; spread over cheesecake. Cut cheesecake into 16 slices. Purée raspberries (strain seeds, if desired). Stir in 2 tablespoons of Amaretto. Top each serving with 1-2 tablespoons of raspberry mixture.

Stanford Inn by the Sea

The Stanford Inn by the Sea embodies the best of the rugged Mendocino Coast. Rather than an inn with gardens, this is a small, working organic garden and farm with an inn. Yet, in the tradition of the finest inns, it offers superior guest accommodation with views of the gardens, pastures and ocean.

Most rooms have wood-burning fireplaces or wood stoves, works by local artists and country antiques. Relax in pine- and redwood-paneled rooms with four-poster or sleigh beds and sitting areas. Most rooms offer stunning views of Mendocino Bay and the Pacific Ocean beyond.

INNKEEPERS:	Jeff & Joan Stanford
ADDRESS:	44850 Comptche Ukiah Road
	Mendocino, California 95460
TELEPHONE:	(707) 937-5615; (800) 331-8884
E-MAIL:	stanford@stanfordinn.com
WEBSITE:	www.stanfordinn.com
ROOMS:	32 Rooms; 9 Suites; Private baths
CHILDREN:	Welcome
ANIMALS:	Welcome; Resident dogs, cats, llamas & horses
HANDICAPPED:	Handicapped accessible
DIETARY NEEDS:	Will accommodate guests' special dietary needs

Vegan Chocolate Torte

Makes 1 (10-inch) Torte

"This excellent, dairy-free torte is our most popular dessert." ~ Innkeeper, Stanford Inn By the Sea

Filling:
1¼	pounds soft silken tofu*
1¼	cups water
1½	teaspoons vanilla extract
¾	cup evaporated cane juice or sugar
½	pound semi-sweet chocolate, chopped
¼	cup sugar

Pinch of salt

Crust:
½	cup chopped walnuts, toasted
¼	cup canola oil
¼	cup milled cane sugar or brown sugar
¼	teaspoon salt
¼	teaspoon baking powder
¼	cup unsweetened cocoa powder
1	cup all-purpose flour

For the filling: Combine tofu, water, vanilla and evaporated cane juice in a large, heavy saucepan. Bring to a boil, lower heat and simmer until liquid reduces and tofu turns light brown. In a double boiler, melt chocolate. In a blender, blend tofu mixture, melted chocolate, sugar and salt until smooth.

For the crust: Preheat oven to 350°F. In a food processor, process walnuts until fine. With processor running, add oil. Add sugar, salt, baking powder and cocoa; process to combine. Add flour; process to combine. Transfer to a bowl and blend with hands until mixture is a uniform color and texture. Press dough into a 10-inch tart pan. Bake for 15-20 minutes (be careful not to burn crust). Pour tofu mixture into crust, chill thoroughly and serve.

*Note: Silken tofu has a soft, silky texture. It is available in the dairy section of most groceries.

Dennen's Victorian Farmhouse

Dennen's Victorian Farmhouse was built in 1877. The inn offers affordable luxury, from elegant linens, feather beds and fluffy towels to an incredible gourmet breakfast served to your room. Breakfasts may consist of quiches, stratas, eggs Benedict, streudels, frittatas, homemade muffins and breads and the inn's signature coffee.

Just minutes away, the historic village of Mendocino offers an eclectic mix of art galleries, shops, restaurants, museums and performing arts, set amidst the old New England charm of wooden walkways and picket fences.

INNKEEPERS:	Jo Bradley & Fred Cox
ADDRESS:	7001 North Highway One
	Little River, California 95460
TELEPHONE:	(707) 937-0697; (800) 264-4723
E-MAIL:	frednjo@victorianfarmhouse.com
WEBSITE:	www.victorianfarmhouse.com
ROOMS:	9 Rooms; 2 Suites; 1 Cottage; Private baths
CHILDREN:	Children age 12 and older welcome
ANIMALS:	Not allowed
HANDICAPPED:	Handicapped accessible
DIETARY NEEDS:	Will accommodate guests' special dietary needs

Best Friends Chocolate Cake

Makes 1 Cake

"My best friend gave me this recipe years ago. It is something we still share often and is a family favorite. It's a deliciously chocolatey cake that can stand on its own, even without the coffee drizzle or, the recipe can be doubled and made as a layer cake. The cake is vegan and is great for people with dairy or egg allergies – though you'd never know it!" ~ Innkeeper, Dennen's Victorian Farmhouse

1½   cups all-purpose flour
¼   cup unsweetened cocoa powder
1   cup sugar
Dash of salt
1   teaspoon baking soda
1   cup water
5   tablespoons vegetable oil
1   tablespoon white vinegar
1   teaspoon vanilla extract
¼   cup raisins, flaked coconut, chocolate chips and/or walnuts (any 1 or a mixture of any or all totalling ¼ cup), or more to your taste
Ice cream, for serving (optional)

Coffee drizzle topping:
1   teaspoon instant coffee powder
Powdered sugar
2   tablespoons boiling water, about

Preheat oven to 350°F. Grease and flour a 9x9-inch baking pan. In a large bowl, combine flour, cocoa, sugar, salt and baking soda; mix well. Add water, oil, vinegar and vanilla; mix well. Stir in raisins, coconut, chocolate chips and/or walnuts. Pour batter into pan. Bake for 30 minutes, or until a toothpick inserted in center comes out clean. Cool cake briefly, then poke holes in it with a fork or a toothpick. Pour topping over cake. Serve warm or at room temperature with ice cream. Great with coffee and a best friend.

For the coffee drizzle topping: Combine coffee powder, powdered sugar and enough boiling water to form a drizzling consistency.

Blackthorne Inn

Blackthorne Inn Bed & Breakfast provides intimate accommodations in a rustic, beautiful setting adjacent to the magnificent Point Reyes National Seashore and an hour from San Francisco and the Wine Country. The unique structure resembles a giant, elegant treehouse. Crafted from redwood, cedar and a 180-foot Douglas fir cut and milled on-site, the four-level inn rises through fragrant trees to sunny decks.

A generous buffet breakfast is served on the deck or in the glass solarium whose walls were once doors in the old San Francisco railroad depot.

INNKEEPERS:	Susan & Bill Wigert
ADDRESS:	266 Vallejo Avenue
	Inverness, California 94937
TELEPHONE:	(415) 663-8621
E-MAIL:	susan@blackthorneinn.com
WEBSITE:	www.blackthorneinn.com
ROOMS:	5 Rooms; 1 Suites; Private baths
CHILDREN:	Children age 14 and older welcome
ANIMALS:	Not allowed
HANDICAPPED:	Not handicapped accessible
DIETARY NEEDS:	Will accommodate guests' special dietary needs

Fudge Ribbon Cake

Makes 12 to 16 Servings

2	tablespoons plus 1 stick butter, softened
¼	cup plus 2 cups sugar
1	(8-ounce) package cream cheese, softened
1	tablespoon cornstarch
3	eggs, divided
2	tablespoons plus 1⅓ cups milk, divided
1½	teaspoons vanilla extract, divided
1½	cups all-purpose flour
1	teaspoon salt
1	teaspoon baking powder
1	teaspoon baking soda
4	ounces unsweetened baking chocolate, melted

Chocolate frosting:

¼	cup milk, plus more if needed
½	stick butter
1	cup chocolate chips
1	teaspoon vanilla extract
2½	cups powdered sugar, sifted

Preheat oven to 350°F. In a small bowl, cream 2 tablespoons of butter, ¼ cup of sugar, cream cheese and cornstarch. Add 1 egg, 2 tablespoons of milk and ½ teaspoon of vanilla; beat with a mixer at high speed until smooth and creamy. In a large bowl, combine flour, 2 cups of sugar, salt, baking powder and baking soda. Add 1 stick of butter and 1 cup of milk. Beat well at low speed. Add remaining ⅓ cup of milk, 2 eggs, chocolate and remaining 1 teaspoon of vanilla; beat at low speed for 90 seconds. Spread ½ of batter in a greased and floured 9x13-inch baking pan. Carefully spread cream cheese mixture over batter. Top with remaining batter. Bake for 50-60 minutes, or until a toothpick inserted in center comes out clean. Cool cake, then frost.

For the frosting: Combine milk and butter in a saucepan over medium heat. Bring to a boil, then remove from heat and stir in chocolate chips until melted and combined. Stir in vanilla and powdered sugar. Beat until smooth. Thin with a few more drops of milk, if needed.

Castle in the Clouds

Situated on eight acres in the heart of Napa Valley, Castle in the Clouds Bed & Breakfast offers easy access to fine dining and wine tasting. Look down from the house upon world famous wineries including Silver Oak, Opus One, Harlan Estate, Mondavi, Far Niente and more. Enjoy a full breakfast, down comforters, deluxe robes and the best views in Napa Valley.

The Honeymoon Suite has fireplace, king-size bed and jetted tub. The room is decorated with antique French furniture, Oriental rugs and original art and has spectacular views of Napa Valley through the bay window.

INNKEEPERS:	Jean & Larry Grunewald
ADDRESS:	7400 St. Helena Highway 29
	Napa Valley, California 94558
TELEPHONE:	(707) 944-2785
E-MAIL:	larry@castleintheclouds.com
WEBSITE:	www.castleintheclouds.com
ROOMS:	3 Rooms; 1 Suite; Private baths
CHILDREN:	Children age 12 and older welcome
ANIMALS:	Not allowed
HANDICAPPED:	Not handicapped accessible
DIETARY NEEDS:	Will accommodate guests' special dietary needs

Avery's Rum Cake

Makes 9 Servings

"We serve this cake for afternoon tea or as an evening snack." ~ Innkeeper, Castle in the Clouds Bed & Breakfast

½   cup chopped pecans
Maraschino cherries (optional)
1   (18½-ounce) package butter recipe golden cake mix
1   (3½-ounce) package vanilla instant pudding mix
4   eggs
½   cup light rum
½   cup water
½   cup vegetable oil

Hot rum glaze:
1   cup sugar
1   stick butter
¼   cup rum
¼   cup water

Preheat oven to 325°F. Grease and flour a Bundt pan. Sprinkle nuts in pan. Put Maraschino cherries around bottom of pan, if desired. In a large bowl, combine cake and pudding mix. Add eggs, rum, water, and oil; mix for 2 minutes. Pour batter into pan. Bake for 60 minutes, or until a toothpick inserted in center comes out clean. Remove cake from oven. Poke holes in top of cake with a toothpick. Immediately pour hot glaze over cake (cake will settle). Cool cake in pan for 30 minutes, then remove cake from pan, slice and serve.

For the glaze: Combine sugar, butter, rum and water in a small saucepan over medium-high heat. Bring to a boil and boil for 2-3 minutes.

Mine House Inn

The Mine House Inn Bed & Breakfast is a peaceful oasis located in the heart of the Gold Country. Gold Rush history, Victorian-era antiques and modern amenities combine to create a welcome retreat from the hustle and bustle of everyday life.

Each meticulously decorated room in the main building features authentic 19th-century antiques and all have private entrances. The rooms are named after their original functions in the historic Keystone Mining Office.

INNKEEPERS:	Allen & Rose Mendy
ADDRESS:	14125 State Highway 49
	Amador City, California 95601
TELEPHONE:	(209) 267-5900; (800) 646-3473
E-MAIL:	minehouse@cdepot.net
WEBSITE:	www.minehouseinn.com
ROOMS:	8 Rooms; 5 Suites; Private baths
CHILDREN:	Children age 14 and older welcome
ANIMALS:	Not allowed
HANDICAPPED:	Handicapped accessible
DIETARY NEEDS:	Will accommodate guests' special dietary needs

Orange Pumpkin Poppy Seed Cake

Makes 12 to 16 Servings

"This is great for breakfast, brunch or dessert." - Innkeeper, Mine House Inn

1	(18-ounce) package yellow cake mix
1¼	cups canned pumpkin
⅔	cup orange juice
3	eggs
¼	cup poppy seeds

Preheat oven to 350°F. Grease and flour a 9-inch (12-cup) fluted tube cake pan. Beat cake mix, pumpkin, orange juice and eggs with a mixer on low speed for 30 seconds, then beat on medium speed for 2 minutes. Add poppy seeds and mix until blended. Bake cake for 35-45 minutes, until a toothpick inserted in center comes out clean. Cool in pan for 10 minutes, then invert cake onto a wire rack and cool completely.

The Upham Hotel

The Upham Victorian Hotel & Garden Cottages is situated on an acre of gardens in the heart of downtown Santa Barbara, a red tile, white adobe, flower-decked town evoking romanticized Spanish California. The hotel is the oldest continuously operating hostelry in Southern California.

San Francisco Focus magazine awarded the Upham Hotel its California Grand Hotel Award for the "Best Small Hotel in Southern California." Louie's, the hotel's restaurant, features California cuisine and has been nationally recognized by *Travel & Leisure* magazine.

INNKEEPERS:	Jan Martin Winn
ADDRESS:	1404 De La Vina Street
	Santa Barbara, California 93101
TELEPHONE:	(805) 962-0058; (800) 727-0876
E-MAIL:	upham.hotel@verizon.net
WEBSITE:	www.uphamhotel.com
ROOMS:	37 Rooms; 5 Suites; 8 Cottages; Private baths
CHILDREN:	Welcome
ANIMALS:	Not allowed
HANDICAPPED:	Handicapped accessible; Call ahead
DIETARY NEEDS:	Will accommodate guests' special dietary needs

Orange Cream Cheese Pound Cake

Makes 1 Bundt Cake or 2 Loaves

2	sticks butter, softened
1	(8-ounce) package cream cheese, softened
1	unpeeled orange, quartered
1½	cups sugar
4	eggs
2	teaspoons vanilla extract
2½	cups all-purpose flour
2	teaspoons baking soda
¼	teaspoon salt
2	tablespoons sour cream

Orange icing:

1	cup powdered sugar
2-5	tablespoons orange juice

Preheat oven to 350°F. In a large bowl, cream butter and cream cheese with a mixer on medium speed. Chop orange to fine pieces in a food processor. Add chopped orange and sugar to butter mixture; beat for about 2 minutes, until fluffy. Add eggs, 1 at a time, beating well after each addition. Beat in vanilla. In a medium bowl, combine flour, baking soda and salt; add to butter mixture and beat until smooth. Add sour cream and beat until well combined.

Pour batter into a greased Bundt pan or 2 (9x5-inch) loaf pans. Bake for 55-60 minutes, until a toothpick inserted in center comes out clean. Cool cake in pan for 5 minutes, then remove from pan and cool completely. Drizzle with orange icing, slice and serve.

For the icing: Mix powdered sugar and enough orange juice to form a drizzling consistency. Mix until smooth.

The Historic National Hotel

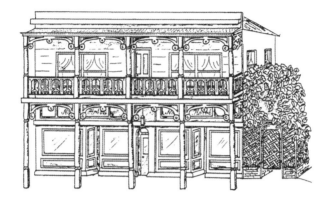

Located in Jamestown, halfway between Yosemite National Park and Lake Tahoe, this historic, California Gold Country bed & breakfast was established in 1859 and is one of the oldest continuously operating hotels in the state. Each of the award-winning, restored rooms has a wonderful brass bed, regal comforters, lace curtains and a private bath.

The highly acclaimed National Hotel Restaurant has both indoor and outdoor seating in the European style. The restaurant's award-winning wine list features selections from the Sierra Nevada foothill wine region.

INNKEEPERS:	Stephen Willey
ADDRESS:	18183 Main Street
	Jamestown, California 95327
TELEPHONE:	(209) 984-3446; (800) 894-3446
E-MAIL:	info@national-hotel.com
WEBSITE:	www.national-hotel.com
ROOMS:	9 Rooms; Private baths
CHILDREN:	Children age 10 and older welcome
ANIMALS:	Dogs & cats welcome
HANDICAPPED:	Not handicapped accessible
DIETARY NEEDS:	Will accommodate guests' special dietary needs

Praline Flambé Dessert

Makes 1 Serving

Plan ahead – this dessert needs to be made 24 hours in advance.

Praline candy:

1	cup light Karo syrup
3	tablespoons butter
1	cup sugar
1¼	teaspoons baking soda
2	tablespoons chopped nuts

Chocolate covered bonbons:

2	ounces semi-sweet chocolate
1	teaspoon vegetable oil
2	scoops vanilla ice cream

Apricot flambé:

1½	tablespoons butter
1	tablespoon brown sugar
3	apricots, halved
½	teaspoon brandy

For the pralines: In a saucepan, bring Karo syrup, butter and sugar to a boil. Watch for color to change to a very light brown (260°F on a candy thermometer); remove from heat. Add baking soda; stir very rapidly, then pour onto a buttered baking sheet. Sprinkle with nuts; spread nuts toward edges of pan. Cool, then break into pieces and freeze in a sealable plastic bag.

For the bonbons: Heat chocolate and oil until melted and combined. Cool for 20 minutes, then spoon over ice cream balls, coating well. Freeze bonbons in a sealable plastic container.

For the flambé: Melt butter in a skillet over medium heat. Stir in brown sugar. When sugar is melted and starting to bubble, add apricots. Cook for about 30 seconds, then remove from heat. Pour brandy over apricots. Return to heat. Carefully light brandy with a long match and cook off alcohol. Reduce sauce to desired consistency. Pour sauce over bonbons. Top with praline candy to serve.

Geographical Listing of Bed & Breakfasts

Central Coast & Valley

Gold Country & High Sierra

Northern California

Alphabetical Listing of Bed & Breakfasts

Index

EXPERIENCE A ROOM WITH A DIFFERENT VIEW

Three great ways to get to know the Inns of *California*

FREE ONLINE NEWSLETTER — INN*crowd*

Featuring Seasonal Specials, CABBI Gift Certificates, Travel Tips, Recipes and much more!

Each month, The InnCrowd features useful information about the many uses and advantages for staying at a distinctive CABBI bed & breakfast inn. From tips for planning a family gathering to finding that last minute getaway, this exclusive online newsletter will help you discover a new travel experience awaiting you at more than 300 state-wide CABBI B&B inns.

To sign up for this free newsletter, please visit www.cabbi.com/signup.

CABBI GIFT CERTIFICATES

Celebrate life's celebrations with the gift of travel. CABBI gift certificates are perfect for weddings, anniversaries, birthdays, and other special occasions. Available in any dollar amount, CABBI gift certificates are versatile and can be redeemed at hundreds of inns throughout California (individual inn policies apply). Gift certificates have no expiration date and can be redeemed at the participating inn of your recipient's choice. Call (800) 284-4667 or visit www.cabbi.com for more information.

FREE CABBI TRAVEL GUIDE

CABBI is California's largest tourism organization representing the bed and breakfast industry; with over 300 B&Bs and inns throughout California. All CABBI properties are inspected and certified, and adhere to a 68-point quality standard ensuring that guests experience consistent customer service, amenities, and the convenience of choice.

To order our *FREE TRAVEL GUIDE* containing over 300 Bed & Breakfasts and Country Inns throughout California,

- Send a self-addressed, stamped envelope to:
  CABBI, 2715 Porter Street, Suite 104, Soquel, CA 95073

- or visit **www.cabbi.com/guide** and order it online.

Can't wait for the Travel Guide? Visit www.cabbi.com and search for inns by region, city, amenities, and availability. You can also access each CABBI member's website through www.cabbi.com.

California Association of Bed & Breakfast Inns

CABBI.com

(800) 284-4667 · www.cabbi.com

The Bed & Breakfast Cookbook Series

Entertain with ease and flair! B&B's and Country Inns from across the nation share their best and most requested recipes. More than just a recipe collection, each book in the Bed & Breakfast Cookbook Series will help you choose the perfect B&B for your next getaway.

California Bed & Breakfast Cookbook
From the Warmth & Hospitality of 127 B&B's and Country Inns throughout California. Book #5 in the series.
$19.95 / 328pp / ISBN 1-889593-11-7

Colorado Bed & Breakfast Cookbook
From the Warmth & Hospitality of 88 Colorado B&B's and Country Inns. Book #1 in the series! New 2nd Edition.
$19.95 / 320pp / ISBN 0-9653751-0-2

New England Bed & Breakfast Cookbook
From the Warmth & Hospitality of 107 B&B's and Country Inns in CT, MA, ME, NH, RI & VT. Book #6 in the series.
$19.95 / 320pp / ISBN 1-889593-12-5

Texas Bed & Breakfast Cookbook
From the Warmth & Hospitality of 70 B&B's, Guest Ranches and Country Inns throughout the Lone Star State. Book #3 in the series.
$19.95 / 320pp / ISBN 1-889593-07-9

Virginia Bed & Breakfast Cookbook
From the Warmth & Hospitality of 76 Virginia B&B's and Country Inns. Book #4 in the series.
$19.95 / 320pp / ISBN 1-889593-09-5

Washington State Bed & Breakfast Cookbook
From the Warmth & Hospitality of 72 Washington State B&B's and Country Inns. Book #2 in the series. New 2nd Edition.
$19.95 / 320pp / ISBN 1-889593-05-2

✳ Coming Soon: *North Carolina Bed & Breakfast Cookbook* (Fall, 2004) and *Georgia Bed & Breakfast Cookbook* and *New York Bed & Breakfast Cookbook* (Spring, 2005). ✳

Bed & Breakfast Cookbook Series
Order Form

655 BROADWAY, SUITE 560, DENVER, CO 80203
888.456.3607 • www.3dpress.net • orders@3dpress.net

PLEASE SEND ME:	Price	Quantity
CALIFORNIA BED & BREAKFAST COOKBOOK	$19.95	_____
COLORADO BED & BREAKFAST COOKBOOK	$19.95	_____
NEW ENGLAND BED & BREAKFAST COOKBOOK	$19.95	_____
NORTH CAROLINA BED & BREAKFAST COOKBOOK	$19.95	_____
TEXAS BED & BREAKFAST COOKBOOK	$19.95	_____
VIRGINIA BED & BREAKFAST COOKBOOK	$19.95	_____
WASHINGTON STATE BED & BREAKFAST COOKBOOK	$19.95	_____

SUBTOTAL: $ _____

Colorado residents add 3.8% sales tax. Denver residents add 7.2% $ _____

Add $5.00 for shipping for 1st book, add $1 for each additional $ _____

TOTAL ENCLOSED: $ _____

*Special offer: Buy any 2 books in the series and take a 10% discount.
Buy 4 or more books and take a 25% discount!

SEND TO:

Name _____

Address_____

City _____State _____Zip _____

Phone_____A gift from: _____

We accept checks, money orders, Visa or Mastercard. Please make checks payable to 3D Press, Inc.

Please charge my   ☐ VISA   ☐ MASTERCARD

Card Number _____Expiration Date_____